SIGHING FOR
EDEN

SIGHING FOR EDEN

SIN, EVIL & THE CHRISTIAN FAITH

WILLIAM H. WILLIMON

Abingdon Press
Nashville

Sighing for Eden

Library of Congress Cataloging in Publication Data

WILLIMON, WILLIAM H., 1947–
　　Sighing for Eden.
　　Includes Index.
　　1. Theodicy. 2. Good and Evil. 3. Sin. 4. Providence and
government of God. 5. Suffering—Religious aspects—Christianity. I. Title.
BT160.W55　　1985　　231'.8　　84-14555

ISBN 0-687-38447-8

Manufactured by the Parthenon Press at
Nashville, Tennessee, United States of America

TO
THE STUDENTS
AT DUKE UNIVERSITY

CORRUPTION

Sure, It was so. Man in those early days
   Was not all stone, and Earth,
He shin'd a little, and by those weak Rays
   Had some glimpse of his birth.
He saw Heaven o'er his head, and knew from whence
   He came (condemned,) hither,
And, as first Love draws strongest, so from hence
   His mind sure progress'd thither.
Things here were strange unto him: Swet, and till
   All was a thorn, or weed,
Nor did those last, but (like himself,) dyed still
   As soon as they did Seed,
They seem'd to quarrel with him; for that Act
   That fel him, foyl'd them all,
He drew the Curse upon the world, and Crackt
   The whole frame with his fall.
This made him long for home, as loath to stay
   With murmurers, and foes;
He sigh'd for Eden, and would often say
   Ah! what bright days were those?
Nor was Heav'n cold unto him; for each day

The valley, or the Mountain
Afforded visits, and still Paradise lay
  In some green shade, or fountain.
Angels lay Leiger here; Each Bush, and Cel,
  Each Oke, and high-way knew them,
Walk but the fields, or sit down at some wel,
  And he was sure to view them.
Almighty Love! where art thou now? mad man
  Sits down, and freezeth on,
He raves, and swears to stir nor fire, nor fan,
  But bids the thread be spun.
I see, thy Curtains are Close-drawn; Thy bow
  Looks dim too in the Cloud,
Sin triumphs still, and man is sunk below
  The Center, and his shrowd;
All's in deep sleep, and night; Thick darknes lyes
  And hatcheth o'er thy people;
But hark! what trumpets that? what Angel cries
  Arise! Thrust in thy sickle.

—Henry Vaughan

CONTENTS

FOREWORD
PARADISE LOST

May is the best month to be alive in Greenville. The azaleas, which begin to bud before Easter, are still in full, radiant bloom. Trees are fresh green and the white dogwoods that line North Main Street and McDaniel Avenue are perfect complement to the fine, columned homes and well-kept yards there.

My life began on May 15, 1946, in this southern Eden. The world's greatest war was over and Greenville, bustling city of the New South, boasted forty thousand inhabitants who were ready to cash in on peace in mid-May 1947 as I was just learning to walk on a pine-shaded lawn south of town.

Greenville lies in the foothills of the Carolina Piedmont. It boasts the world's purest water, which comes cascading down the blue mountains to the north of the city. The air is also pure in Greenville, particularly in May when the need for coal heat has long since passed in the little clapboard houses that surround Greenville's textile mills to the west of town. The mills were built during the last century just outside the city limits where taxes were lower, so they and their poor, tallow-skinned, mill village inhabitants do not deface the pleasing picture of Main Street in spring.

An early landowner named McBee gave Greenville's first Christians free land on the town's four corners. From here, tall-steepled Presbyterian, Baptist, Methodist, and Episcopal churches preside over the city. I was brought to the Methodist of these churches for baptism. Therefore, in mid-May of 1947, having ended the first year of my life, taking my first hesitant steps on the lawn of my ancestral home, I was, as yet, innocent and pure.

Nineteen forty-seven would be remembered in Greenville for more significant events than my first birthday. On February 15, a white taxi driver named Tom Brown picked up a black passenger, Willie Earle, who asked to be driven to his mother's home in Pickens County, eighteen miles from Greenville. Unknown to these two men of different races, they had something in common. The Fates had dealt with both in similarly tragic ways. Earle, born to a fourteen-year-old mother on a poor tenant farm, had worked for a time as a truck driver. But Willie Earle was an epileptic. His employer discovered this when Earle had a seizure at work and fired him. Subsequently, Earle became depressed and began to drink heavily. His moodiness turned to violence when he assaulted a white construction supervisor on the job. He was sent to the state penitentiary for a year or so. A short time after his release, he hailed Brown's taxi one February night for a fateful ride into the country.

Tom Brown's life was also tragic. He mustered out of the First World War with a serious injury that rendered him unable to do strenuous work; therefore, he had taken a job as a taxi driver—work which was considered demeaning by Greenville society. Brown was known as a kindly, generous man, a good influence on the seedy "taxi boys."

No one will know precisely what happened between the black man and the white man out on S.C. Route 63 that night. Shortly after midnight, Willie Earle reached his home on foot. A passerby found Brown dying from deep knife wounds, choking in his own blood, lying beside his taxi, a mile or so from Earle's home. Police quickly arrested Earle and incarcerated him in the small, antiquated Pickens County Jail. Brown, in mortal agony, was taken to the hospital in Greenville.

Late the next night, a crowd of angry taxi drivers assembled at the Blue Bird Taxi Company located, ironically, behind the hideous yellow brick Greenville County Court House. In the darkness of a cold February night, voices grew in intensity and liquor was passed around for fortification. Engines were started; men pushed into a dozen taxis and headed west, out of town and toward Pickens. A neon sign on the insurance building across from the now quiet and deserted Blue Bird Taxi Company blinked on and off the words *Liberty Life.*

Though the Greenville Sheriff's Office was located on the bottom floor of the courthouse, only a few yards from the cab company, nobody there seemed to notice the assemblage. Sometime before dawn, a crowd of fifty men arrived in Pickens in taxis and forced the aged jailer to hand over Willie Earle. This the old man did without protest except to ask that the men use no profanity since his wife lay sleeping upstairs.

"I guess you boys know what you're doing," the jailer said, as the taxi drivers led Willie Earle out into the darkened, empty streets of Pickens.

Just before dawn, someone called the black mortician in Greenville and told him, "There is a dead nigger in need of your services by a slaughter pen on Highway 63." Willie Earle's mutilated body was found in the open field, just as the caller had said, near the slaughter pen. He had been beaten, stabbed repeatedly, and shot a number of times at close range in the body and head. The bushes around his body were splattered with brain tissue and blood.

At about the same time that Willie Earle's tortured

body was found, Tom Brown breathed his agonized last breath at the hospital as the first light dawned on a frosty Greenville mid-winter morning.

Within days after the lynching, thirty-one men were arrested. The FBI took conflicting statements from each of the men, statements which would be little help to the prosecution. A broken shotgun was presented as evidence, broken, it was said, while Willie Earle was being beaten to death.

In the same ugly yellow brick County Court House behind which the mob had assembled in February, a trial began in May. A jury was selected, an all-white jury of thirteen men—textile workers, a couple of salesmen, a farmer, a mechanic, and a truck driver.

During the two-week trial, the town stood center stage in the national press. Major newspapers sent reporters to Greenville. Rebecca West became famous for her *New Yorker* article on the trial entitled "Opera in Greenville."

The prosecution and the defense were led by lawyers from the best of Greenville gentry. The courtroom was presided over by a southern gentleman of a judge who quoted poetry and demanded that the trial show the nation that the South was civilized. But the antics of both the prosecution and the defense were often less than dignified. Reporter West noted, "The Bible belonging to Greenville County Court House is in terrible shape. . . . Its quietest hours are when it is being sworn upon; at any other time, it is likely to be snatched up . . . , waved in the air, held to an attorney's breast, thrust out over the jury box, and hurled back to its resting place in a convulsion of religious ecstasy." All done, West noted, with the intention of impressing a jury who are assumed to be both religiously pious and ignorant.

At one point in the trial, a defense attorney told the jury that he failed to see why a man would be prosecuted for shooting a "mad dog"; the man should be "honored by the community for ridding it of a dangerous menace."

The lawyer was reprimanded, but the members of the jury got his point. On May 12, 1947, three days before my first birthday, they handed down a verdict: not guilty. The end of what *Life* magazine called "the nation's greatest lynch trial" was greeted by most of the white citizens of Greenville with a sigh of relief. Few black people expected anything other than acquittal; they had been through it all before. Tom Wofford, defense attorney, commented that "the solution is education for both races." Far away, the Minneapolis *Times* declared, "The spirit of Justice is dead in Greenville, South Carolina, and its citizens live in the shadows of a great shame."

Thirteen years later, I received my Eagle Scout Award in the same room where thirty-one men were tried by the people of Greenville for the murder of Willie Earle and declared innocent.

ONE

EAST OF EDEN

I want to tell a story, a true story. That is, a story that really happened, is happening, and will happen. I warn you here at the beginning, that, being a true story, it is a story involving evil—the other side of life, the dark side, the chaos underneath the order of this world. It is a story about sin, sickness, violence, war, and even the little, everyday, ordinary cruelties we inflict upon others and ourselves and which, in turn, are inflicted upon us out here, east of Eden.

But how shall we tell such a thing except in whispers, except with fear and trembling? For we are narrating the shadow side of ourselves. This is the side that most of us do not want to hear about at all, the part of our world that we dare not think about too often or too long. It is good to be cautious in our tales about this for we are entering dark waters which quickly become deep and treacherous to the soul. Before we know it, we could be in over our heads.

So why think about such somber matters at all? Why enter this cancer ward of the world? Why turn off the pleasant flower-lined autobahn to Munich and detour toward the hell called Dachau? Why climb Golgotha and look at the world from the Place of the Skull? Why not focus upon the good news rather than dwell on the bad? Why peer into the secret, ugly, "rag and bone shop" of the heart when there is so much about you and me to be affirmed as good?

In general, this has been exactly the point of view of American theology and church life down through the years. On the whole we are an optimistic, progressive, positive people who want to believe the best about ourselves. Prophets of doom and purveyors of bleak Calvinism have never been heard gladly in our culture. We want to hear about Horatio Alger and Pollyanna and success stories that end happily ever after.

For us, evil is something unpleasant that happens to other people, something of the Old World that our forebears left behind when they immigrated to this arcadian paradise. Human nature, the average American believes, is basically good. Sure, we have our faults, make our mistakes, but, down deep, we are at heart decent people who are doing the best we can.

Little wonder, then, that American theology and church life have tended to be optimistic, self- and world-affirming, and convinced that, given the proper environment, education, and advantages, we will all become better and better, nicer and nicer. We are a people who march behind the banner of positive thinking, self-affirmation, human potential, and upward mobility for all. Who dare suggest that our alleged goodness is merely a sham, our cheerful optimism but a façade behind which we have stashed the ugly clutter of a side of human nature we are too fearful to admit?

This book goes against the grain in saying that evil is a reality of life which cannot be denied, a fact of a fallen world which we cannot ignore. First, we talk about evil because it is a genuine portion of reality. Whatever we say about the world we are in, whatever claims we make for the human race, we have not told the whole story until we speak of this other side of goodness.

Second, as Christians, we talk about evil because, until we have confronted it, we have not raised the fundamental questions for which the story of Christ is (for us) the only satisfactory answer.

Third, we talk about evil as Christians because in telling this tale there are practical consequences for Christian education, pastoral care, preaching, worship, ethics, social action, and all other aspects of our life together in the family of God.

So how shall we talk about this disturbing reality? In this book I shall reflect upon evil through stories—my story, which involves being born in Greenville in a world of Willie Earle and Tom Brown; God's stories, which involve people like Adam and Eve, Cain and Abel, David and Bathsheba; and the story which makes all these other stories intelligible and bearable, the story involving Jesus of Nazareth. It is my conviction that these stories make me who I am and reveal the truth about the evil in me and in the world in a way which is both truthful and redemptive. My hope in telling these stories is that you will see your own story in these and even come to see the story of Jesus as your own.

For good and for ill, I was born in Greenville.

I know that this may not strike you as particularly significant. Many contemporary people see themselves as ahistorical, without family, place, tradition, or stories—I choose to be whom I want to be. I am a self-made person, alone, liberated, free, choosing my identity and destiny.

And so an out-of-the-closet homosexual sings "I Am What I Am"—a paean to modern identity—in the musical *La Cage aux Folles:*

> I am my own special creation . . .
> It's my world
> That I wanna have a little pride in.

Personal maturity is thus defined as the heroic attempt to fabricate "my world." *My* world. Americans tend to think of growing up as leaving home, putting aside Mama and Daddy, overcoming background, severing roots, and choosing some new, self-selected identity. You "find yourself" sometime between nineteen and twenty-five by jumping on a Honda and heading West for a year or paying fifty dollars for two afternoons of psychotherapy. You are whomever you want to be. Your story is whatever explanation you create for yourself.

Many people who grow up in South Carolina are full of strange and inaccurate ideas. But the modern fiction that we are without roots, history, and an inheritance is not one of them. I have an accent, some stories, and a point of view, all of which remind me that I did not choose to be who I am. I have come from somewhere, put here in spite of what I may have wanted. Any wisdom I hope to be given in this life must come to terms with where I have come from and therefore who I am. To know anyone else who tells different stories is not to know me.

So to say that I was born in Greenville is to say that my life is constituted by a narrative which describes me as a coherent, identifiable self. Your stories are your way of taking hold of the world and making you who you are. Therefore, it is important to try to tell our stories as truthfully and accurately as we can, for the truth or falsehood of our lives will be shaped accordingly.

I hope to show that being born in Greenville and telling and living these stories help me better understand the Christian story. My story illuminates aspects of the Jesus story that I might have missed had I not heard that story as someone who was born in Greenville, in the world of Willie Earle and Tom Brown.

But you object and say, "The story I read at the beginning about the murder of Willie Earle and the succeeding trial had nothing to do with you at all. At the time this drama of life and death was being enacted, your greatest concern was how to put one foot in front of the other without dropping your diaper."

How is this story my story?

It is my story because I am like the ancient Hebrews who preserved and recounted the biblical tales of creation, exodus, exile, sin, and redemption. Their stories characterized who they were, made sense out of their place in the world, and located them within a saga which gave purpose to their lives. Abraham's story was their story as children of Abraham.

To be a Jew is to be someone who responds to the query of the young by recounting:

> We were Pharaoh's slaves in Egypt; and the LORD brought us out of Egypt with a mighty hand; and the LORD showed signs and wonders, great and grievous, against Egypt and against Pharaoh and all his household, before our eyes; and he brought us out from there, that he might bring us in and give us the land which he swore to give to our fathers. (Deuteronomy 6:21-23)

Thus, at Passover, around the family dinner table, the Jewish child asks, "Why is this night special above all other nights?" And the father replies in all accuracy, "We were Pharaoh's slaves in Egypt, and the Lord our God brought us forth from there with a mighty hand and an outstretched arm. And if the Holy One, blessed be he, had not brought our forefathers forth from Egypt, then we, our children, and our children's children would still be Pharaoh's slaves in Egypt.

"So, even though all of us were wise, all of us full of understanding, all of us elders, all of us knowing in the Torah, we should still be under the commandment to tell the story of the departure from Egypt."

We were slaves. We, your great-grandmothers and fathers, were slaves; you were and would be still had not the Lord brought them—you—out with a mighty hand.

Thus, at Passover, to be a Jew is to be one who tells these ancient tales as one's own. They happened, still happen to us. We are those who are inextricably tied to these ancestors, values, and place of the story.

21

So it was for me in Greenville. To be who I am means to be what my family was: living on the same land since the late 1700s, sending some of our kin off to the Civil War to fight Yankees, welcoming them back from the carnage to desperate poverty, living poor but fiercely proud and even vain. In our world you could be proud even though you were poor if you had land, a name, education. From the beginning we were led to believe that the name Willimon—a corruption of the original German—meant something.

Years later my sister would note that, whereas her friends left home with the admonition to "act like somebody," she left home with the charge, "You are somebody."

It was an area in which I could point to the places where my great-great-grandparents had lived down the road a piece. I could tell you where they buried their silver when the Yankees came through on a raid during the war. I had forebears who worked hard, bowed to nobody, and went to college—even the women—and thus were somebody. I was born in a rock house which my mother designed and my father had built from the chimneys of over twenty ruined tenant cabins whose occupants had long since fled red clay and pine hills for the mills of the New South. These rock walls stood to remind me that our people once worked and were responsible for the welfare of twenty families. Such were the roots of my tribe, a lively, proud, Methodist, resourceful, potentially cantankerous, mysterious, ordinary folk who bear this name.

But, of course, this isn't the whole story. I must also tell some of the parts that were left out—that are even more significant because of their omission—the other, unspoken but real part of the tale which I knew by heart. For Greenville is in South Carolina, which means, of course, a place where people were once bought and sold. One afternoon, while rummaging through an old drawer, I came across a bill of sale for "ONE NEGRO MALE" for

"THE SUM OF ONE HUNDRED DOLLARS" signed by my great-grandfather Pack.

My family, I was later told, had only a handful of slaves. Actually, few white southerners ever owned them. But still . . .

There could be other stories told of growing up in a world of white and black, a curious mix of well-defined lines of separation alongside daily and friendly interaction of the races. The Greenville city buses that carried me to town displayed prominent signs reading:

S.C. LAW
WHITE PATRONS SIT FROM FRONT
COLORED PATRONS SIT FROM THE REAR

My friends and playmates, the only children whom I really knew, at least to the age of nine or ten, were people who could not enter our house through the front door.

So there is no escape from this part of the story, the part that is so hard to tell. Yet this is the story of injustice which I perpetuated and benefited from and was, in turn, marked by as much as I was marked by the story of the good. The tough task of becoming a whole person involves telling the whole story—the failures, cruelties, and the tragedies as well as the goodness. The truth of any story is measured, in part, by how accurately it narrates the full drama of what it means to be human.

This brings me back to a cold February night in 1947 and the deaths of Willie Earle and Tom Brown, a story known to me only by way of cryptic, fleeting reference to the "taxi drivers' lynching." Nobody told me this story as I was growing up in Greenville, nor did I ask anyone to.

I did not pursue it until my fourteenth year when, whiling away a Saturday afternoon in the decaying, columned Greenville Public Library, I asked the white-haired librarian to help me find information about the trial. She returned with a file of clippings, a yellowing

New Yorker article by Rebecca West, and other material.
I sat there and read it all.

Someone once asked Carlyle Marney, "Where is the Garden of Eden?"

Marney replied, "Two-fifteen Elm Street, Knoxville, Tennessee."

"You're lying," the person said. "It's supposed to be someplace in Asia."

"Well, you couldn't prove it by me," Marney said. "For there, on Elm Street, when I was but a boy, I stole a quarter out of my Mama's purse and went down to the store and bought me some candy and I ate it and then I was so ashamed that I came back and hid in the closet. It was there that she found me and asked, 'Where are you? Why are you hiding? What have you done?' "

So, two hours after the librarian gave me the file on the lynching of Willie Earle, she tapped me on the shoulder and told me that the library was closing. By that time I had read enough for a large chapter of my own life to be closing, too. What I knew but did not know about my world, I knew then. The lush, primal, secure, arcadian garden had suddenly overgrown with thorns. Serpents did all the talking now. I had eaten of the Tree of the Knowledge of Good and Evil. I had learned from what sort of people I had come. I had heard the whole story, lost my innocence, my ignorance, my purity.

Now, embarrassed by my nakedness, I crept cautiously out of the library and headed back home a different person—fallen, sadder but so much wiser, grown up, eyes opened, driven out of bright Eden by cherubim with a flaming sword.

TWO
THE PROBLEM OF EVIL

Lynching had a long history in America. Before 1890, most lynchings were whites hanging whites. But in the latter part of the century, lynching became a peculiarly racist form of violence. Since then, there are 3,445 cases of blacks being lynched by whites, mostly in the American South.

So this was simply one more—one of the last, fortunately—story of the lynching of a black man by white men.

But because the story of the Greenville lynching and subsequent trial is true and because it is my story, it is revealing in its own way.

As stories of violence go, there is little new or unusual about this episode. But then, is evil ever original or creative in its manifestations? Any account of the outburst of evil is invariably the same old, very old story. The story of Willie Earle is reenacted today, with appalling sameness, anywhere people gather.

Further, since this is a story of evil, it would be nice to find some villain in the tale, someone to pin it on, some convenient criminal. Who here is the villain? In all probability, Willie Earle stabbed Brown and left him to suffocate in his own blood that night. But Earle was as much victim as villain, the violent, dispossessed product of a violent, racist society. He was a murderer, yes, but hardly the source of the larger evil.

At first hearing, the white taxi drivers are likely candidates for the role of villains in the story. But, even as Willie Earle was an oppressed black man, the drivers could be similarly dismissed as oppressed whites. They were also products of a system which put them at the bottom of society. "White trash," they were called. Poor, uneducated, recently returned from a world war where they were drafted to take a gun and blow off some German or Japanese head, they were now expected to reenter civilian life in a world no more free or democratic than when they left to fight a war to preserve it. True villains, the ones we love to hate, should be made of uglier stuff.

So we could point beyond these unfortunate men, seated row upon row in the hot, crowded courtroom, in their tight, cheap suits, with their reddened, oily faces sweating in fear. We could point beyond them to the "system." Yes, the system—that must be the real source of evil in this case. The system with its university-educated lawyers who guard the establishment and its interests. These were the ruling class who praised those who took a troublesome nigger out and taught him a lesson last year but now, with the attorney general and northern newspapers breathing down their necks and with this being bad for business, now they call it murder and conspiracy and say somebody has to hang for it.

They too—the judges, lawyers, reporters—they too are not only beneficiaries of the system but also its victims, the ones who now must explain a land that sacrificed thousands of its youth to stop the Fascists who killed Jews so that we could be free to stomp to death a poor, ignorant epileptic like Willie Earle.

And even the cadre of reporters who, after moralizing about the great injustice of the trial and its verdict, took the next train north, returning to New York, Minneapolis, or Detroit in self-righteous indignation, even they were implicated. At least the folk, black and white, who stayed behind to pick up the pieces and go on living in Greenville had been made to view something down deep about themselves that the enlightened northerners had yet to see, could not see until years later when they and their sons had a little night ride of their own in the rice paddies of Vietnam.

There is something a bit hollow about Rebecca West's *New Yorker* piece on the trial. One can imagine her urbane readers getting a chuckle over the backwardness of the red-necked, white-linen-suited lawyers and their lint-head defendants, then turning the page to peruse advertisements of the latest offerings at Tiffany's. It was well for them to be reassured by Miss West that *New Yorker* readers are above this sort of impropriety. It can't happen here.

And wouldn't it have been good if Tom Wofford's comment had been right, that "the solution is education for both races"? But surely he knew that it is a much deeper problem than that. It is a problem implicating all races, classes, and sexes, and it is more perplexing than the failure of an inadequate educational system. It is the problem of being human and not being able to do one blessed thing about it except to lynch, kill, blame, accuse, lie, and suffer, trapped in our own stupid B-grade movie of a tragedy that we have seen enacted a hundred times before, more victims than villains, caged animals, dying every day, wishing to God it were not so but it is, oh, it is.

Evil as a Problem for Believers

"There is greater suffering and misery in the world than at any time in human history," pronounced the World Council of Churches after its Vancouver Assembly. The statement was probably made for effect rather than accuracy, for it is patently untrue. Who could tell the victims of centuries of famine, plague, wars, sickness, and injustice that our world is more miserable than theirs? Masses of human beings have always lived in conditions where food, health, clothing, safety, and shelter were limited and suffering was a part of everyday life. Admittedly, our technological progress has been an ambiguous phenomenon, creating new problems even as it solves old ones. While wars, political injustice, and human hurt continue in the modern age, we have made some progress.

And yet we are among the first generation to realize the painful limits of human progress. As we entered this century, scientific advances heralded the advent of a new era. The scientist became the high priest of beneficent modernism, unlocking the mysteries behind disease, bad weather, and natural disaster. Freud probed the mind and raised the possibility that mental illness and human psychic anguish could be "cured." The telephone, the incandescent light, the radio, the auto, the airplane linked us to one another and shrank the world into a global village where improved communication and transportation would lead to a new international harmony. Technology was our panacea. We would all ride into a bright future on the back of a smoothly running machine that would make life easier, longer, and happier for all.

Today, standing at the end of this century, we wonder how anyone could have believed such romantic rubbish. The idea of progress through science, technology, or psychotherapy wins few adherents today. Only politicians of the Right or of the Left still pay homage to the notion. We now know what our forebears did not. The same X-ray that helps the surgeon also causes cancer. "Miracle drugs" can produce horrible diseases. The telephone, radio, and airplane were not a way to a new humanity, but tools that enabled the barbaric efficiency of the Nazis. Whereas their tyrannical predecessors could handle only a few thousand victims at a time, Hitler, Stalin, and Mao found science the willing ally of a new barbarism that could smoothly exterminate millions. Whatever happened to the mighty atom that was to be "harnessed for peace"? The psychotherapy of Freud could be used as well for brainwashing and "therapy" for Soviet political dissidents as for the curing of neuroses.

So, if we today are not more miserable, perhaps we are more aware of our limits in eradicating evil and its attendant miseries than in the past. Television news makes us instantly, vividly aware of evil. Vietnam was not the worst or most morally questionable war the United States has fought. It was the first war we fought from our living rooms at 6:30 P.M.

Now, under the shadow of the mushroom cloud, with humanity inched ever closer not toward progress but rather toward the Dark Ages of nuclear oblivion, evil presses itself upon us in new, cosmic proportions. More than ever, we need to know all we can about our darker side. More than ever, we need to be utterly honest about the danger of our situation. We are not making progress. In fact, we stand upon the threshold of a nuclear abyss which makes us ask again all the old questions about human nature, the future, sin, evil, and morality; this time with new earnestness.

More than a decade ago, while I was in my first parish, The Exorcist was playing to packed movie theaters. This rather trashy tale of demons, priests, and possession swept the nation. The South Carolina Academy of Religion asked me to be a panelist in a discussion of The Exorcist and its appeal. One by one, the religion professors analyzed the movie as a last vestige of outmoded theism in reverse, a rather nonsensical outpouring of popular religious ignorance.

I took another view. "Isn't it odd," I said, "that having been assured by us clerics that the devil doesn't exist, that evil is something archaic which we have overcome, that

29

sin is a figment of our imagination—people pay good money to see a movie like this?"

In spite of what we good liberal theologians told them, people still experienced evil within their own lives. In spite of our reassurances, they continued to feel something like the demonic at work in their world, some dark, unmentionable, irrational terror at the heart of things that caused a chill to go down their spines. What a pity—their churches no longer spoke of such subjects. Only the movies, in their usual, superficial way, dared deal with evil.

When theologians refuse to speak of evil and sin, people go to horror movies. When biblical scholars cease thinking in apocalyptic terms, people read science fiction. When the Roman Empire was crumbling, Augustine reflected upon eschatology. When the Black Death was sweeping Europe, Christian artists and preachers turned their thoughts toward the torments of hell. Today, when utter annihilation is as near as the push of a button, it is perverse *not* to be somewhat preoccupied with human perversity. *Gross exageration*

[margin handwritten note: haven't people always done these things regardless of what pastors + leaders do to say?]

Evil as a "God Problem"

How shall we think about evil? Philosophers commonly speak of the "problem of evil." Problems are for solving. But the concrete experience of evil—a serious illness, the death of a child, a hurricane, the face of a starving mother—strikes us as an outrage rather than a problem. The victim of evil is typically not a philosopher. Rather, the victim is rendered incapable of thought—weeping, screaming, withdrawing in numbed silence, or crouching, like a wounded animal, in fear.

[margin handwritten note: Are these things evil?]

Pastors quickly learn that when someone is in the midst of a great tragedy, she usually does not want adept citation of Scripture, sermonettes on the will of God, or philosophical analysis. What she wants most is an empathetic tear, a firm hand upon the shoulder, our quiet reassurance that we know and we care.

And yet pastors also know that if all we have to offer the sufferer is an empathetic tear, a firm hand upon the shoulder, we offer very little in the long run. In the immediate crisis of grief or pain, our quiet presence may be enough. But the trouble with human suffering is that it doesn't end there. Presumably, animals experience tragedy, say, the loss of their young, and rebound in a relatively short time. On our farm we separated calves from their mothers a few months after birth. The cow would bawl for a couple of hours in a way that was akin to human maternal feelings. But by the next day, cow and calf seemed unaffected by the separation, so far as I could tell.

We humans are different. After the tears are over—sometimes before they are over—we want to know *why*. We shake our fists and cry out in the darkness. We refuse not to ask questions. All the empathetic comments and reassuring pats on the shoulder do not keep us from thinking about evil and wondering from whence it came and for what purpose it exists.

Therefore every philosophy, every theology, every human being must take account of evil. I never met a person who did not have a well-developed philosophy of evil—whether that person knew he or she had it or not. Of course, some try to avoid the problem by declaring that evil doesn't exist. As great a mind as Emerson's could assert that evil is only an idea that is the result of an uninformed way of looking at things. If we would only focus upon the good, if we were wise enough to see the picture as a whole, we would see that what appears to us as evil is only an element of the larger good. Mary Baker Eddy founded a church on the notion that what we feel as pain isn't really pain if we just get our heads straight. But this sanguine optimism does not wash when

Not Avoidance!

Maybe Emerson was right.

Miracles.

She was on right track.

He cannot conclude what "works" for everyone.

confronted by evil, not as a philosophical exercise, but as concrete, personal manifestation. Few facts of human experience are any more real, any less illusory, any better documented by history, than the presence of evil. One can find much within human life that is hard to comprehend, but evil is as accessible as the front page on the morning newspaper.

Little wonder then, that our best minds—particularly our best Christian minds—have turned themselves toward a consideration of this problem, because the problem of evil strikes at the very core of the Christian faith. Aquinas said that the presence of evil was one of the two main stumbling blocks to belief in God. More recently, Hans Küng calls evil the very "rock of atheism." Richard Rubenstein, in *After Auschwitz*, says that after Hitler's death camps, the continued belief in a God of love who acts for the good of his people is utterly nonsensical. On the whole, the historic question has been not, Is there a God? but rather, Is God good?

This continues to be the conventional challenge of the skeptic. I heard it only the other night while visiting a man who had been inactive in our church for a number of years. I assumed that his inactivity was due either to sloth or to his disenchantment with our congregation. He told me that his problem was "deeper than that."

"I just can't believe in God when there is so much pain and suffering in the world," he said.

His comment suggested that he was an "intellectual," someone who dared to think about deep, weighty matters. At least he is intellectual enough to know that this is the one question sure to silence even a loquacious preacher. More than this, it suggested that he was a morally sensitive person.

I could question his moral sensitivity—sitting there in his hundred-thousand-dollar home in a segregated, affluent suburb of Greenville. But this might be unfair.

Here was a questioning, troubled soul who saw evil as the central problem to belief in God.

Though he did not know it, his dilemma was nothing new. In "On Evil" in his *Dialogues Concerning Natural Religion,* David Hume long ago reformulated Lucretius' challenge to faith:

"Is He [God] willing to prevent evil, but not able? then is He impotent. Is He able, but not willing? then is He malevolent. Is He both able and willing? whence then is evil?"

The Judeo-Christian heritage affirms the goodness and omnipotence of God. And yet, there is this evil in the world. How do we account for that? Does God permit evil to be here? Then God must be something less than good. Is God just as upset by evil as we are yet unable to eradicate it from the very world God is believed to have created? Then God must be something less than omnipotent. So the argument goes.

What are we to make of a world which God made and, according to the Genesis account, declared to be "very good," and yet seems saturated with so much pain and heartache? Even the most determined back-to-nature freak living on an organic farm in Vermont must at times, say, when watching a mother hog systematically devour her young, agree with John Stuart Mill's charge that "nearly all the things which men are hanged or imprisoned for doing to one another, are nature's every day performances."

What is a believer to say to such a challenge? Here is the "Satan" (literally, the "accuser") who perpetually accuses the Christian faith of grave inconsistencies in logic. "Where is your God?" the scoffer asks the suffering believer (Psalm 42:9-10).

As John Hick notes, evil is not a problem for all religions; only for those religions which claim that the god they worship is perfectly good and unlimitedly powerful. Biblical faith is such a religion. One can try to ease out of the dilemma by attempting to show that God is not unlimitedly powerful. Some contemporary theologies have done this. Later I shall argue that when they deny God's omnipotence, they are describing a god who is not the God of Abraham, Isaac, Jacob, and Jesus. This God, this all-loving and all-powerful God, is the God for whom, in our human minds at least, evil is a "problem."

 The conventional Christian way of thinking about the problem of evil is called *theodicy*. *Theodicy* comes from the Greek *theos*, "God," and *ieke*, "justice." Theodicy is the philosophical attempt to justify the ways of God to humanity, an attempt to think about what God does with evil and why.

Immediately, we may be put off by the whole enterprise. First, we are referring to evil as a "problem." Problems are for solving. We therefore can be expected to use our best human wit to solve this problem of God and evil in an attempt to set things right, doing so with more than a touch of defensiveness. Does evil lend itself to such philosophical gymnastics? Knowing how we are accustomed to think about things, we can be expected to be overly rational about the alleged "problem," to fit this essentially irrational, utterly mysterious and devastating phenomenon into some logical straitjacket which we can manage. Can we do that with evil, the evil that terrifies us the most, and still be honestly talking about evil? Isn't it somewhat immoral for us to sit back in our padded armchairs and think calmly about suffering? Dare we call such coldhearted logic *compassion*? Might the most moral response to the world's *Why*? be a long, honest pause followed by a humble, "I don't know why and it scares me to death"?

Second, is it not a foolish pretension on the part of a finite creature to presume to "justify the ways of God to humanity"? How can we possibly judge God by human standards of what is right and wrong?

34

For my thoughts are not your thoughts,
  neither are your ways my ways, says the LORD.
For as the heavens are higher than the earth,
  so are my ways higher than your ways
  and my thoughts than your thoughts. (Isaiah 55:8-9)

Perhaps my energy as a pastor should be better expended in justifying the ways of sinful humanity to God or, better, to be silent like Job (in the end) before incomprehensible mystery.

But is this a fair restriction upon our thought about God? Is evil the one unmentionable subject for theology? Perhaps I, as a pastor, should take the advice I received in seminary pastoral counseling courses. When ministering to my people who are sick, dying, bereaved, or victimized, I should simply embrace them, be with them, and try to share their hurt and pain. I remember a young seminarian who described for some of us his encounter with a young father whose child had just died of a horrible disease.

"Chaplain," the man said, "I can't understand why this happened. We have always gone to church. Why did God do this?"

"What did you say to the man?" we asked.

"Say? Why, nothing. I don't believe that there are answers to such questions. I've learned in my Clinical Pastoral Education course that a minister shouldn't preach at people. I should simply share their pain, absorb it."

Well, yes. I see his point. But the grieving father did ask a straightforward question to which presumably a pastor, while not having all the answers, might have a few answers. In three years of seminary, all this young man had learned was that he was to be silent and plead sympathetic ignorance. This response implied that (1) the man's question was nonsensical or impious, and (2) the Christian faith has no response.

I believe that pastors are called by the church to

35

respond to such questions. To fail to respond is to abandon my office as pastor and therefore as teacher, theologian, and preacher. I am called not only to empathize but also to interpret, to reflect, and to proclaim. Evil is an intellectual problem no less than an emotional one.

"My God, why?" is a profoundly intellectual question. As John Hick notes, evil is a "problem" only for the spectator, not for the sufferer. The sufferer's problem is how to survive, how to keep one's head above chaos. But eventually most sufferers, if they survive, become spectators and ask *why?*

So we back away from these questions only through a kind of intellectual cowardice, moral insensitivity, or smug self-centeredness that says, "There, but for the grace of God, go I." As a pastor, as a Christian, I can't do that without forsaking my vocation. The grieving father has a point: If God presides over a world where little children suffer and die before their lives have a chance to begin, why worship this God?

There will be those cheerful souls who deny that evil is such a fierce problem for the believer. Evil, they say, as bad as it is, is ultimately balanced by good. Why not focus on all the good in life rather than morbidly dwell upon momentary ugliness?

My own story suggests that evil is more than a sporadic intrusion into life. Something about life at its base, right at the center of things, is full of ugliness. I daresay the facts of history, sociology, and psychology, when these disciplines have dared to be true to their own research, give empirical support for this view.

Harry Emerson Fosdick once said that the good in the world was a greater challenge to the skeptic than evil was to the believer. How does the atheist explain the presence of genuinely good people and genuinely good deeds without reference to God, the supreme instigator of such goodness?

36

John Hick reminds Fosdick that the atheist is not at pains to explain anything. If you are not convinced of the existence of an all-loving, all-powerful God, you are not under obligation to account for the *why* of good or bad, or the purpose and meaning of anything else, for that matter.

Only the Christian need be concerned about these mysteries. Only the believer could comprehend what my friend Stuart Henry means by his declaration that, when he stands one day face-to-face with the Almighty, he shall thrust forth a cancerous bone and cry, "Why? O God, why?"

hardly!

THREE
AUGUSTINIAN THEODICY

One way to go forward is to go backward. Thus, I try to understand what it means to be an adult by recovering an episode from my childhood. What has been said about evil in the past?

Traditional theodicies which attempt to "justify the ways of God to humanity" go in one of two directions: (1) *Augustinian theodicy*, which sees a "fall" from a state of primal innocence into sin and evil and our subsequent rescue by God, and (2) *developmental theodicy*, which sees today's sin and evil as a stage in a long development in which God shall eventually work out everything for good. The Augustinians try to make sense out of evil by looking backward, the developmentalists by looking forward. This chapter shall examine how Augustine deals with sin and evil.

Early in his life, Augustine (d. 430) was attracted to Manichaeism. Adherents of this rather esoteric mythology saw the world as a place of constant conflict between good and evil. We experience this cosmic warfare right in our own hearts, say the Manichaeans. Flesh and spirit are always in tension. God is the good which eternally struggles against evil and strengthens us in our battles with this dark adversary.

Many of us still think in dualistic, Manichaean terms, dividing our world into two opposing camps. The person who says, "The devil made me do it," is thinking dualistically, like a Manichaean. The human soul often feels like a battleground where lust, bad thoughts, and dark inclinations war with what we sometimes refer to as "our better nature." Sometimes we divide the world into "evil" Communists and "good" Americans who shall never be reconciled because one is wholly evil, the other wholly good. The U. S. president calls the Soviets "the evil empire"; the Soviet president responds that the U. S. "violates the elementary norms of decency." Only a final nuclear cataclysm shall end this struggle.

Dualism—the ancient Manichaean variety or its modern imitators—continues to be so popular because this is the way evil often feels. The teenager who, troubled by his sexual feelings, pledges to God not to think any more "dirty thoughts," is inevitably perplexed by his total inability to keep his vow for more than thirty minutes. It is as if something or someone is inside of him, tugging at his good intentions, dragging him down. The devil must be making him think these terrible thoughts.

When Augustine converted to Christianity, he rejected his Manichaeism because it could not be reconciled with the Judeo-Christian notion of an all-powerful and all-loving God. Augustine asked how God could be omnipotent and yet permit evil to rampage through the world. Is the devil equal in power to God, so powerful that God is unable to do anything about evil? If God alone is all-powerful yet still permits the devil to do mischief, then God must be ultimately responsible for the continued existence of evil.

Augustine's theodicy attempted to solve this dilemma by placing responsibility for evil solely upon the shoulders of humanity. In *The Freedom of the Will*, Augustine notes that Genesis says that humanity is created "in the image of God" (Genesis 1:27). This means, says Augustine, that men and women are created in the image of God's *freedom*. (It is interesting that Augustine picked freedom as the distinguishing trait of the divine rather than love or creativity or righteousness. The Genesis story does not spell out the substance of this "image.")

For Augustine, the human situation is the result of freedom misused. Adam could have chosen good. Unfortunately he chose bad, and it has been hell ever since. If Adam and his heirs misused their freedom and rebelled, only humanity can be held accountable.

But this idea simply pushed the problem a step further back for Augustine. If Adam chose the bad rather than the good, how did the bad arise in the first place? Surely God must have had some hand in its creation or at least permitted it presence.

Augustine responds by dividing the problem into two levels. Evil entered the cosmos through the free deviation from God's good intentions by the rebellion of Satan. Thus, Augustine attempts to explain why this demonic adversary is abroad in the world without implicating God.

Human evil is caused not by rebellious angels but rather by Adam's freely chosen deviation. What happened in Eden parallels what had happened in heaven. The sin of *pride* leads us to rebel, to haughtily turn from the joy God intends for us as children of God in our attempts to be gods unto ourselves. We were created for bliss, creatures who were, in our freedom, the very image of God. Yet we turned away from the bliss of Eden and were driven out of the garden. There is no cause for this within ourselves, no created flaw within us or evil within the external environment. So our fall cannot be blamed upon God. It is the human misuse of a divine good gift of freedom which brings us to grief.

Augustine rejected the Manichaean idea that matter, the world, was evil, that our bodily nature consigned us to sin. Such dualism contradicted the plain testimony of Genesis, which claimed that God looked upon the creation and declared that it was "very good" (Genesis 1:31).

On the Nature of the Good was Augustine's exploration of the idea of good and bad. Dualism assigns evil to two different powers which are almost equal to each other. Like the black-and-white tesserae of a mosaic, good and evil, as opposites, make up the pattern of our world.

Augustine said this wasn't so. The black stones are flaws, defects of the good rather than independent realities. A bad person isn't a demon, a subhuman being. That person is a warped specimen of humanity. Disease is not some independent reality. Disease is a breakdown of health just as darkness is the absence of light.

Thus, for Augustine, evil is a lack or "privation" of good. Creation, as the work of a good creator, is intrinsically good. A major aspect of goodness is *order.* Augustine borrows from Platonic philosophy in seeing creation as a hierarchical organization, a "great chain of being" with God at the top, humanity a little lower than God, all the way down to the seemingly insignificant animals and insects. Every created thing in this great chain has certain God-given limits, form, and order. Goodness is the result of living happily within one's proper sphere, in harmonious relationship with those creatures above and below.

The trouble starts when some being aspires to a structure which is higher than its appropriate level, such as an ape desiring to be a man; or conversely, when a being becomes enamored of a lower level, say, when man acts like an ape. This pridefully denies one's proper, harmonious goodness; disfigures the orderly beauty of creation; destroys harmony; and introduces chaos.

Augustine says this happened in Eden. Unsure about the duration of their primal bliss, Adam and Eve got too big for their britches, ate of the forbidden fruit, and upset

41

the balance. Wrong choices lead to evil. Evil is perversion of the created order.

Augustine said some uncomplimentary things about sexuality. But what he said was based upon his reading of Genesis 1:28, where the man and woman are told to "be fruitful and multiply." Sex is proper and beautiful— when used as an act of procreation. It is disgusting and demonic when used as an act of pure pleasure because this is not its appropriate function, its proper goodness.

The ancient notion of a "great chain of being" was upset by Darwin, who showed that nature, rather than being a fixed hierarchy of creatures, is in constant flux and development, with species rising, disappearing, changing. Natural selection assures that no species remains fixed in its set place on the "chain," but rather is in a process of evolution. What Augustine would have made of evolution, we know not; however, it raises a fundamental problem for our acceptance of his world view.

What about those other circumstances of nature which we commonly refer to as "evil" but are not due to human choice—floods, hurricanes, and natural disasters? Augustine distinguishes between various kinds of evil.

1. First, there is evil which human beings originate through the wrong exercise of human freedom. This includes all human actions which we call sinful—cruel, unjust, perverse behavior. This he calls *moral evil.*

2. Second, there is *natural evil.* Natural evil originates independent of human action—disease, earthquakes, storms. Augustine's elaboration of human free will does not really help to justify natural evil.

3. Third, there is what he calls *metaphysical evil.* This is related to the basic fact of human finitude. We sometimes speak of our inevitable death, the passage of time, and old age as being evil, as causing us pain and regret. But these are natural limitations of our being human and not being divine.

Augustinian theodicy traces all evils, including moral and natural evil, to this ultimate cause. We were created "in the image of God," but we were also created as animals, not as angels. When we rebel against our situation, moral evil is the usual result. Adam was fine until he realized that his bliss might not last. When Adam tried to take matters in his own hands and escape his humanity, he lost his higher, rightful, blissful fellowship with God and fell into sin.

Likewise, the things that we call natural evil are usually the result of orderly processes of nature which come crashing down upon us. It is not necessarily "evil" that a rock falls from a cliff and rolls onto a highway. The rock is simply acting in accord with gravity, a law we rely upon and enjoy. But if we should be traveling down the road and the rock crushes us, this "orderly process of nature" will seem evil indeed. Augustine thus implies that our definition of evil may be the result of our human inability to see the whole picture.

The Augustinian notion that evil is a part of the larger picture of overall good has been called "aesthetic." That is, in the sight of God, many aspects of life which we consider repugnant, unfair, and unwarranted—even sin and its consequences—combine to form a beautiful harmony which is ultimately very good. If there were no bad, then we would not know what was good, just as we would not know light without darkness, health without illness, Augustine says.

Consistent with his definition of evil as "privation of the good," and his conviction that everything fits into an orderly, harmonious scheme of things, Augustine was loath to admit that there are aspects of life which are completely, unredeemably evil.

Everything, even the misfortunes of life, has its rightful place in the order of creation. As the weavers of oriental carpets tie the knots, sometimes they make mistakes. Rather than ripping out their mistakes, the skilled artists incorporate the mistakes into new patterns, bringing good out of "evil," until, in the end, each carpet is uniquely beautiful and interesting.

Augustine says that when we cry out that this or that is unjust, we are like ignorant people who complain that a painting is not beautiful because the small patch of color we are focusing on at the moment is not beautiful. Or we are like dimwits who criticize a drama because every moment of the play is not interesting or all of the characters are not heroes but include fools and clowns. By the end of the last act in a great drama, we see that even the seemingly pointless and unattractive parts have contributed to the whole. We must be patient because, with the Lord, "a thousand years [is] as one day" (II Peter 3:8).

Criticism

One has the feeling, after reading Augustine, that everything is just a bit too tidy in his theodicy. Too much is explained with too much dexterity and impersonality. How much comfort would it be to tell Willie Earle that his death contributed to some as yet unknown good in the long run? In admiring the alleged harmony of the universe, Augustine loses sight of its ugly disorder. One can understand how the sacrifices and struggle of four years of college contributed to the larger good of a well-paying job, or how the pain suffered in an operation was worth it in order to rid the body of a cancerous tumor. But too much evil is excessive, gratuitous, and, by any reasonable estimate, pointless.

The facts of human existence do not support the notion of evil as aesthetic imbalance, "privation of good." Evil often displays a distinctive, independent, and terrifying power. Could one stand out by the slaughter pen as a group of thirty ordinary men beat in the head of Willie Earle and say that what we have here, as this juggernaut of violence picks up tempo and engulfs everyone, are

44

Are we to say they are basically evil people who occasionally show a hint of goodness?

AUGUSTINIAN THEODICY

basically good people in whom evil was a bit more present than good on this evening?

The folk who stood in line waiting to see *The Exorcist* knew—evil is not merely the absence of kindness but a terrifying, demonic force. *with mind of its own?*

Nor does the Bible depict evil, as does Augustine, as metaphysical substance. In the Bible sin is a personal, ethical act, a breach in the divine-human relationship. Divine grace is not a substance that repairs an imbalance in human character, filling us with a little more good. Grace is a loving restoration of the divine-human relationship.

The advent of Jesus Christ is not the infusion of goodness to put a misguided world back on course; it is the arrival of a *person*. Here is a God who relates to us in an utterly personal, incarnate, engaging way.

In his attempt to use Neoplatonism to justify the ways of God to humanity, Augustine fails to keep close to the story. We must speak about God, not by imposing certain acceptable human qualities such as freedom, harmony, or order upon God, but rather by listening attentively to the story. "In Christ God was reconciling the world to himself" (II Corinthians 5:19). So we must observe Jesus' way with people as a sign of God's way with people. Jesus established not aesthetic perfection or natural harmony, but communion. His governing principles, as John Hick notes, were ethical rather than aesthetic.

In the Old Testament, God is not some perfect force which sets things in harmony and then lets nature work its course. God creates, loves, forgives, chooses, liberates. Jesus' stories tell of God as a loving parent who loves his human children individually and seeks them like a shepherd searches for the lost sheep, a thrifty woman searches for a lost coin, or a good father waits for a lost boy.

The story of the lost boy (Luke 15:11-32) suggests that if the wayward lad had not returned home but had instead

45

been irrevocably lost, the fact that this was the son's own fault and that the harmonious balance of the world was undisturbed would not assuage the father's wounded love.

As John Hick notes, it is difficult to picture this God sitting back with an air of self-satisfaction and noting that, though millions were put through hell and left in hell, the moral balance of the universe is unbroken. If God can grieve over the loss of one sparrow, how must God feel over the loss of a person? Any view of the world that rules out such resourceful, determined, persistent love is less than Christian. Augustine's God is the unmoved mover of the Greeks, the divine watchmaker who sets it all in motion and then lets things happen as they will. This isn't the way the Bible tells it.

If God really wants a beautiful and perfect world, God seems to have missed the mark. Why, with a world so orderly, so harmonious, so perfect, did things get so rotten?

Free Will

Augustine would exculpate God by referring to the free-will defense. Humanity is to blame for all the rottenness because of our tragic misuse of our freedom. We could have used our freedom wisely. Then, presumably, we should still be blissful in Eden rather than sighing out here east of Eden. The cause of evil is a defect in human will. God is innocent, having created good creatures who inexplicably choose wrong.

Yet here is the insurmountable inexplicability. How could this unqualifiedly good creature commit sin? In *The City of God*, Augustine describes Adam and Eve in the garden in the most lavish, idealized terms. How could people be so dumb as to corrupt so paradisical a state? The answer, for Augustine, lay in the misuse of their free will. Yet, by putting all the blame upon the shoulders of humanity, human choice of evil is rendered unintelligible. What on earth could lead perfect people to destroy their idyllic bliss through their rebellion?

Admittedly, the greatest bulk of human suffering is due to our wrong actions, the misuse of our free will. Augustine is right about that. Isn't it interesting, when people bring up the subject of evil, they usually mention what Augustine calls "natural evil" first? How does God explain, they want to know, hurricanes, leukemia, bad weather, and all the other horrors we suffer?

avoidance

But instead of "justifying the ways of God to humanity," perhaps we ought to be more concerned with justifying the ways of sinful humanity to God! Moral evil continues to be the heart of the problem. Many, many patients in American hospitals are there for diseases which are related to alcohol and drug dependence. A doctor told me that two-thirds of his patients suffer from diseases that we know how to cure—if we would only stop smoking, stop drinking, exercise, and eat properly. We do not lack the means or the resources to cure much of the world's poverty and disease. We lack the *will*. No doubt many of these sufferers consider themselves to be under the baffling grip of natural evil. But a sober look suggests that moral evil causes their plight; *sin*, to put it bluntly. We are more responsible for our suffering and the suffering of others than we are willing to admit.

And yet God must also be responsible. If we are sinners, who made us liable to sin? Augustine answers that God desired us to freely love him, not as puppets, but as full, free persons. If we are to be free, we must be truly free to choose either right or wrong.

But granted this, why did God not make us so that we always choose what is right and good? A Calvinist, building as Calvinists do, upon Augustine, might respond that even to ask such a question is vainly to attempt to limit God. God made us this way because God wished it so.

But still, we can't help asking: Why couldn't God

have created us free, but free to choose what is good?

The English philosopher Ninian Smart responds in "Omnipotence, Evil and Supermen" (*Philosophy*, April/July 1961):

> Imagine some perfect being who is created to always do what is right. (Obviously, we are imagining something other than a human being.) Could we say that such a being is "courageous"? Not really, for courage implies that we have overcome fear. But we have said that this perfect being feels no fear or cowardice. This being is immune from such weakness.

Smart's point is that the very notion of good implies that a creature has the possibility of being otherwise—has temptations, real fears, true limitations which must be overcome; otherwise, we could not call this creature either "good" or "free."

Yet couldn't we at least have been created a bit more disposed to do good than evil?

Even this general disposition would hedge our freedom. Real freedom presupposes the possibility of real wrong. A parent who claims to have a "good child" is not telling the whole truth if this "good child" has been so protected and directed that she never really had to choose or to discipline herself to do what was good. If God desires that we should freely, without coercion or fear, come to fellowship, then God cannot guarantee that we will come. Presumably, as the Bible tells it, God not only wants us to obey; God also desires our love and worship. That makes the divine-human relationship risky, unpredictable, and perilous.

Thus God is willing even to allow sin and evil to exist in the world because, in Augustine's words, "God judged it better to bring good out of evil, than to suffer no evil to exist." Later, Aquinas would quote from the Easter liturgy, "O happy sin which merited so great a Redeemer." In the end, God is able, through Christ, to redeem even our rebelliousness and sin.

Yet not for everyone. Augustine observed that some people see the error of their ways (as he did) and turn to God. Some do not. If God is busy using even our imperfections to eventually make a perfect harmony, what about these intractably rebellious ones?

Augustine explains that some people have a knowledge of the good; some do not. Some are "elect"; others are damned. But this hedges on the idea of human freedom, a freedom which Augustine believes is the very essence of our humanity.

When carried to its logical extreme in Calvin's predestination—God wills some to good, some to damnation—questions are raised about the complete goodness and the complete freedom of God.

We are back to the problem of how to absolve God from being implicated as the author, or at least the permitter of human sin and the world's evil. Since this is an intolerable idea for Augustine, we are left with a serious philosophical dilemma.

Augustine took the Greek aesthetic view of the world with its notion of evil as privation of the good and wedded it to the Judeo-Christian sense of sin as personal rebellion against God.

On the whole, Reformers such as Luther and Calvin unquestioningly reasserted Augustinian theodicy, failing to see that his theodicy was not as biblical as they assumed. The sovereignty of God was preserved at the expense of the love and creative freedom of God.

I believe that the Bible depicts a more personal, more dynamic view of God's relations with the world.

FOUR
IRENAEAN THEODICY

Fortunately, in our wrestling with the question of evil, we aren't stuck with only one possible solution. History offers a variety of theodicies—a variety of attempts to "justify the ways of God to humanity."

John Hick rediscovered an early alternative to Augustine's thought on theodicy, Irenaeus of Lyons, a second-century bishop. When Irenaeus listened to the story of Adam and Eve, he heard something different from what Augustine heard. Irenaeus saw Adam and Eve not as perfect, blissful, and innocent beings in the garden, but rather as immature children. Their sin is not damnable revolt and rebellion but rather the result of their weakness and immaturity. Accordingly, their sin calls forth God's compassion more than God's wrath. Adam and Eve are not driven away from God; rather, they are driven, as were all women and men who came after them, into countless new experiences and adventures with God. The Bible is not a tale of how God rejects humanity, washes his hands of the whole rebellious lot, and walks off the stage in disgust. The story—a long story of God's eternal determination to keep working with humanity—begins rather than ends at Eden.

Irenaeus overcomes one of the fundamental problems

50

in Augustinian theodicy. Augustine depicts Adam and Eve as pure, perfect creatures who somehow, quite inexplicably, rebel and fall into sin. Irenaeus sees humanity created immature, with room still left for growth and development, imperfect creatures who await final perfecting by the Creator. *— the perfectibility of man —*

To be created "in the image of God" means that we are raw material for God's continuing and more difficult creative work. God desires not simply that we should be *takes time* perfect, but that we should be in communion, not through coercion but through uncompelled response and willing cooperation.

Our relationship with God takes time. No one can be created in an instant. American evangelical Christianity tends to depict a person's life as "fallen"—caught in sin *Does not believe in* since Adam's fall—then suddenly, instantaneously con- *born again* verted, done over, remade, and restored to perfection in a *perfection* moment of blinding religious experience. But Irenaeus was convinced that the work that God wants to do in us is *to* so great that the result requires a much longer process.

We are talking about the formation of character here, about a relationship with God which matures through time—through a lifetime of response and costly effort, subtle divine promptings, and personal growth. We don't speak of an infant's having "character," for the very notion of character implies a self with a history, an inner consistency which requires time to acquire. While in my own life I can testify to the reality of momentous, instantaneous, deep changes of heart and mind, my own experience confirms Irenaeus' view that human goodness rarely feels like the instantaneous rectification of some primal flaw. Rather, it feels like a gradual building up through a long history and moral effort. A "good person" is that character which is the result of a long process of making good and bad decisions; learning from mistakes; and growing in trust, humility, and insight. This process can be hazardous, full of ups and downs, victories and

51

defeats, for real goodness is not easily achieved.

As Augustine knew, true goodness is related to true freedom, and true freedom entails the possibility of making truly wrong choices. But, with an eye toward the long-term nature of this process which Augustine failed to see, Irenaeus views all these ups and downs, mistakes, and triumphs as necessary aspects of the soul-making process. Our sins, as Irenaeus depicts them, are not so much the result of our stiff-necked rebelliousness, but are rather a necessary aspect of this hazardous adventure in individual freedom. The final result, freely chosen fellowship with God, justifies even the worst tragedies, the darkest sins, and attendant suffering within the process of soul making. Looking back, we will see that the wonderful end result has justified the means.

This notion that the end result justifies the attendant sin, suffering, and difficulty along the way has led to criticism of Irenaean theodicy. Why, we may ask, didn't God simply create a perfect world of perfectly good people rather than put poor humanity through all this?

Those who ask this question, as John Hick notes, are probably imagining some idealistic, hedonistic paradise. Then they criticize God for not creating that imaginary world. They imagine God as if God were the owner of a valuable human pet. If the owner of the pet is truly kind, the owner will build the finest, safest, most comfortable cage for the pet. Any defect in the cage is a bad reflection upon the owner.

But what if God's desire is to have us not as comfortable and contented house pets but rather as beloved children in fellowship and freedom? What if God has created us not simply for comfort but also for development of our character, for depth, wisdom, self-knowledge, and morality? Then what is the best environment for the development of that sort of humanity?

All of us have noted, in common, everyday observation, that people who have a rough time in life are often more complex, interesting, and wise than people who have enjoyed comparatively smooth sailing.

In the churches I have served, people always call on those folk who are the "wounded warriors," who have been dealt blows by life but have endured with dignity and grace. The church is one of the few places where such people are seen as the real heroes of life because the church is attempting to foster a different brand of "success" than that of the world.

The Bible suggests that we are created not for some blissful paradise or for self-sufficient perfection but for fellowship, *koinonia*, communion with God. It is unfair to criticize the world because it is often a place of suffering and pain unless this suffering and pain can be shown to be purposeless.

Consider the analogy which Leslie Weatherhead uses in one of his sermons. A toddler, just learning to walk, trips and falls, cutting his head on the coffee table. The child may think to himself, What cruel and uncaring parents I have, who put me in a situation that causes me hurt and pain.

Yet the cruelest thing of all would be to protect and guard the child to such a degree that the child never learns to walk, never learns to protect himself. Thus Jesus speaks of God as a being a parent, not a beneficent zoo keeper. Parental love at its best seeks to produce children who are free to receive and return love, to foster strength of character and freedom, to decide wisely.

So John Hick comments, "This world must be a place of soul-making. And its value is to be judged, not primarily by the quantity of pleasure and pain occurring in it at any particular moment, but by its fitness for its primary purpose, the purpose of soul-making."

The facts of life in this world are often painful. But we are awaiting nothing less than "a new heaven and a new earth" (Revelation 21:1). Whereas Augustine attempted to understand the presence of evil and suffering by looking backward to an origin in the primordial fall of Adam and Eve, Irenaeus sought understanding by looking forward, by understanding all our difficulties as steps on the path toward a brighter future. He took an eschatological view rather than a historical view. He could say with Paul,

> I consider that the sufferings of this present time are not worth comparing with the glory that is to be revealed to us. For the creation waits with eager longing for the revealing of the sons of God; for the creation was subjected to futility, not of its own will but by the will of him who subjected it in hope; because the creation itself will be set free from its bondage to decay and obtain the glorious liberty of the children of God. We know that the whole creation has been groaning in travail together until now; and not only the creation, but we ourselves, who have the first fruits of the Spirit, groan inwardly as we wait for adoption as sons, the redemption of our bodies. For in this hope we are saved. (Romans 8:18-24a)

Granted all this, one might still ask if so much evil and such horrible suffering are needed to produce good character. The Irenaean response would be that this is an unfair question. The justification for whatever evil we endure is not in the quantity or quality of our trials and tribulations in the present, but the greatness of the good toward which these present tribulations lead in the future. As Paul said, the sufferings of the present age pale into insignificance when compared "with the glory that is to be revealed to us."

Is the end result worth the present price? We must wait and see. Also, we must admit that, in asking such theoretical questions, we are imagining some world that does not exist, peopled by folk who have never existed. Would this imaginary world be better than the world as we know it, even with its pain and sin? Who could answer such a theoretical question?

Developmental Theodicy

Irenaeus' idea that evil is justified only when we are able to stand in the future and look back on how well things have worked out has its counterpart in the developmental, evolutionary thought of later thinkers such as Hegel, Schleiermacher, and more recently, John Hick.

In the eighteenth century, the Augustinian notion that evil, as bad as it was, still somehow served a larger good was pushed to its extreme. The eighteenth century was an age of optimism when new technological advances, the birth of science, and the celebration of reason led to confidence that humanity was really making progress at last. The Dark Ages of superstition and ignorance were behind us; light was dawning; the Enlightenment was in its heyday.

A poet of the period, Joseph Addison (1672–1719), expressed the popular view that the divine gift of reason had at last lifted the clouds from our eyes so that we were now able to see the orderly, congenial cosmos harmoniously ticking around us:

> The spacious firmament on high,
> With all the blue ethereal sky,
> And spangled heavens, a shining frame,
> Their great Original proclaim:
> Th' unwearied sun, from day to day,
> Does his creator's power display,
> And publishes to every land
> The work of an almighty hand.
>
> Soon as the evening shades prevail,
> The moon takes up the wondrous tale,
> And nightly, to the listening earth
> Repeats the story of her birth;
> While all the stars that round her burn,
> And all the planets in their turn,
> Confirm the tidings as they roll,
> And spread the truth from pole to pole.

What tho' in solemn silence all
Move round the dark terrestrial ball?
What tho' no real voice nor sound
Amid the radiant orbs be found?
In reason's ear they all rejoice,
And utter forth a glorious voice;
Forever singing, as they shine,
"The hand that made us is divine."

One nagging problem remained—the problem of evil. If the world was basically a good, orderly, harmonious place, how was one to account for all the bad, disorderly, unharmonious things that happen? Therefore, a major task of intellectuals was theodicy; the attempt to retain the optimism of the age while still accounting for evil.

Some theodicists depicted God as a master clockmaker who fashions a flawless piece of machinery, starts the whole thing in motion, and then lets it run. But what about evils such as storms and sickness? Most theodicies of the age depicted God as a benign underachiever—God is doing the very best he can, but always within the self-imposed limits of natural laws and cosmic forces.

For instance, a man is hit on the head by a falling coconut, causing him much pain. Why did God allow such a thing to happen? he asks himself as he holds his aching head. But what would he have God do? God has created a harmonious world that includes the law of gravity—what goes up, must come down. Surely the man cannot want God to arbitrarily overturn this law, sending the earth hurtling off into space and people flying through the air. A law is a law, even for the God who makes it.

Thus we see that the old Augustinian "aesthetic" view that all evils somehow contribute to the picture of a larger and more beautiful good is reasserted, this time with reference to something called "natural law" which, it is believed, underlies this great perfection.

The more that science uncovers the mysteries of the natural world, the more we shall come to see that those experiences which once seemed so bad were really good. This is the old aesthetic argument of Augustine updated.

The argument works as long as we conceive of God in wholly impersonal terms—as some distant, deistic clockmaker who sets up laws and then lets them work. If a premature infant does not survive, well, that's the "survival of the fittest" principle at work. Bad for the baby, but the species is thereby kept strong. This keeps God out of science's way as it goes about uncovering God's allegedly beneficent laws. But is this the God of the Bible? When a sparrow falls from the air, does God simply note with satisfaction that the law of gravity is still in good working order in this best and most harmonious of all possible worlds?

The notion that this world, as baffling as it may sometimes seem to our uninformed minds, is the "best of all possible worlds" was bitingly satirized in Voltaire's *Candide,* an uproarious tale of a young man who is told by a half-baked philosopher that this is "the best of all possible worlds."

Voltaire takes the young man through a terrible series of calamities—he is beaten and shipwrecked; his wife is assaulted by a regiment of troops. Each time poor Candide picks himself up, brushes himself off, and assures himself, "Well, this is the best of all worlds."

The fatal blow to much of the eighteenth-century optimism came, not from artistic or philosophical attacks like that of Voltaire, but rather from an event of nature—the Lisbon Earthquake of 1755. It is curious how our intellectual houses of cards often come crumbling down, not because of work by intellectuals, but rather through the simple facts of life. I remember a mother who asked me, as a pastor, to speak to her teenage daughter before she left for college and "tell her what we believe so some college professor will not destroy her faith." *Life* is the most severe test of a person's faith; the facts of life itself are threatening enough for belief.

So it was in 1755 that a tremor shook Lisbon and hundreds were killed. This event, while not a massive tragedy by contemporary standards of carnage and destruction, fell like a bombshell upon the pleasant playground of philosophical optimism, somewhat akin to the Holocaust in our own day, shaking the Enlightenment to its core.

In the early nineteenth century, Hegel taught that evil is still somehow a necessary element in the long-term advancement of goodness. For instance, we call diseases such as cancer "evil." Yet at one time we called polio "evil." Today, after human minds have conquered polio with a vaccine, polio means only the slight inconvenience of medication at the beginning of a child's life. Otherwise, it stands as another example of courageous and creative human progress. What kind of world would this be if it were some perfected, hedonistic paradise? There would be no impetus for human growth and development. Thus, even what we call "evil" has its place in the overall picture of human growth.

Hegel's contemporary, Schleiermacher, also urged looking at the full sweep of things before jumping to conclusions about evil. Against Augustine, Schleiermacher said that sin doesn't enter human life back at the "fall" in Eden. Rather, sin breaks into human life, along with goodness, at every moment of life, confronting us with a choice between good and evil. A person's life consists of a million turnings from evil toward good. The challenge is to focus not upon the bad but upon the good. Later, in looking back, we shall see that even our sin has been used by God to bring us closer. I have heard many folk who would agree with Schleiermacher. A friend of mine is deeply convinced that his childhood suffering through rheumatic fever was God's way of forcing him to be a Christian.

A couple in my acquaintance worked and sacrificed to build their "dream house." Two months after they moved in, the house caught fire and burned to the ground. Because they were only partially insured, they were unable to rebuild.

"Well, I guess this is God's way of telling us that we just loved that house more than we loved him," she said, looking back upon the experience.

John Hick acknowledges his debt to Schleiermacher and Irenaeus. Hick's thesis, in a nutshell, is this: Humanity is free—free to come to God. But Irenaeus depicted this movement more accurately than Augustine—as long-term, lifelong turning toward the Creator, involving trial and error, effort and sin, and yes, suffering and pain. If it did not, then there would be no real freedom not to turn to God, no real choice. In order to provide true freedom, God maintains enough distance between himself and humanity to give us room to learn and to grow. Without this distance, human life would have no goal, no reason, no final consummation.

Borrowing a phrase from the poet John Keats, Hick characterizes this world of evil as a "vale of soul-making." This "vale of tears" is also a place where we are being fashioned into the true image which God intends for us in some yet unrealized future.

In Hick's mind, there is no Augustinian "fall" as a historical event. Science now knows that the conditions that caused human disease and mortality and the needs that caused humanity to undertake the labors of hunting and agriculture were part of the natural order prior to the emergence of humanity. All the things we call natural evil—hurricanes, disease, floods—were here from the start.

Second, Hick rejects the notion that everyone is punished for the sin of one man—that Adam and Eve somehow inexplicably rebelled.

As far as Hick is concerned, Irenaeus was right. Humanity, including Adam and Eve, is created immature, with plenty of room left for growth and development. The challenges, obstacles, and even suffering that we encounter as a consequence of living in this world are justified because they are said to evoke the best moral qualities in us. Suffering produces character. The Christian idea of heaven is not simply a place of hedonistic, painless existence. Rather, heaven is a place of fellowship with God. This world is a "vale of soul-making" that prepares us for such a place.

Many would reject Hick's theodicy because they believe that *any* suffering or inconvenience is unjustified. Yet they probably do so out of a fantasy about some hedonistic paradise rather than from a Christian view of final fellowship with God. So their rejection is unwarranted.

There also might be those, even those who are Christian, who feel that, if God wants better people, God ought to make such people, now, in an instant. We live in a world of instant oatmeal, instant dry cleaning, instant this and instant that. We hate to wait. As I said earlier, American evangelical Christianity too often presents the Christian life as an instantaneous event rather than the result of long-term growth and struggle. In classical theological terms, we have overstressed justification (God's work for us in Christ) at the expense of sanctification (our growing response to God). So Hick's stress on the Christian life as gradual, sometimes painful growth seems appropriate.

But like nearly all theodicies of development, Hick's discussion of the positive role of evil in human history is too selective. What about the evil that cannot be explained as a device in human moral development? Certainly a horrible tragedy will sometimes mobilize people to do good. But can all evil be justified on the basis of its possible good consequences?

In his book *God, Why Did You Do That?*, Frederick Sontag suggests that the goodness God wants is so wonderfully excessive that it requires an excessive amount of suffering and pain. And this surely is a logic of development—the greater the good desired, the greater the evil that must be undergone!

Yet most of us are painfully aware that evil has a way of producing even greater evil. An increase in domestic violence usually follows a war—once you take up the gun, it is hard to put it down. Evil can be a stimulus to human advancement, but evil has a numbing effect on people. We come to accept it as normal. Suffering produces despair as often as it produces character. Statistics show that abusive parents are likely to produce children who abuse their children. The violent political revolutions of this century have almost invariably led to new but equally violent repressive regimes.

Moral progress is not evolutionary. The social Darwinians were wrong. Development is not cumulative. Tomorrow's advances often destroy something of yesterday's good. Gains are accompanied by loss. Can a century that produced not just antibiotics, rocket ships, and the United Nations but also Auschwitz and Hiroshima still believe that it is all adding up for the better in the end?

The developmentalists blur distinctions between good and evil since they make evil a virtual necessity for achieving good. Evil almost becomes part of the will of God. But the thing that terrifies us about evil is not the possibility of whether it will or will not all somehow be for the best, but rather the sheer pain of it all, the evil of it all. We call evil "evil" because it terrifies us, threatening to sweep everything in its path, possessing a life of its own, devouring, gaining momentum, crushing out the very life of our souls rather than fortifying our souls. Evil breaks the soul as often as it makes it.

Standing out by the slaughter pen on Highway 63 on that cold, dark night, the broken body of Willie Earle before us, dare we say that this act can be justified as ultimately contributing to some larger good?

In the face of such evil, the possible goods are small change indeed.

V Process Theodicy

Goodness Distorted was how Norman Pittenger's book described the world. Using the concepts of process theology, Pittenger sets human life within the dynamic context of an evolving world which is moving toward fulfillment—which the Christian says is loving communion with God. In each moment of life we decide whether or not to accept this goal of communion and thereby move our lives toward fulfillment. All of us are caught up within this process of the interacting of (to cite another Pittenger book) *Cosmic Love and Human Wrong*.

God is the author of this process. In fact, God is in the process as a loving, persuasive force for good, luring us toward our true destiny. Each of us is a living, dynamic personality in the making. What we experience on an individual level is true on the cosmic and social levels as well. The whole world is evolving toward betterment.

Why do we call an earthquake "evil"? Pittenger wonders. "It is primarily a natural readjustment of the stuff of which the physical world is made, caused (as we are told) by the repatterning that is inevitable on a planet burning hot in the center, cooler on the periphery, and continually contracting." Tidal waves, destructiveness among the animals, even much human pain can be seen as a natural consequence of a world that is still in the process of becoming. Each event presents me, as a free, decision-making creature, with the possibility of decision. Will I open myself to the progress of the world, or will I refuse to be part of this long movement toward goodness?

Comparing human history to a vast river which, though it takes a circuitous path to the sea, at last reaches its goal, Pittenger says that history "makes clear that there *is* a main line of advance, a sound and healthy direction; and when that line is followed, the advance goes forward towards its intended goal."

Where does God come in? Not by direct action or intervention, for that would be unduly coercive. Rather, God acts behind the scenes, persuasively, urging us forward. As for sin, it is a matter of bad choice, "a refusal to follow the sound and right direction of advance" (p. 56). Salvation is "human wholeness or rightness, with the possibility of consistently right decisions among relevant openings" (p. 68).

To uphold all this Pittenger has to range rather far afield from the biblical narrative. Jesus' attitude toward human evil is "not the negative one of condemnation of wrongdoing, it was a positive encouragement and help in their desire to be truly human" (p. 89)—an idea more worthy of Norman Vincent Peale than of the Gospels. In fact, process theodicy is only vestigially Christian, for who needs Christian redemption in this great, good, evolving cosmos?

Process thought on the subject of evil desires to be very scientific. But it is scientific in a rather romantic way. What scientific evidence is there that the evolutionary process of natural selection and survival of the fittest moves toward general betterment? Something may be gained, but something is also lost and the end result may not be cumulatively better. In the end, far too much evil is swept under the rug.

Also, Pittenger's view of human beings, as essentially animals who decide things, is too rationalistic to take account of our psychological complexity. Why on earth do we keep choosing wrong? one asks. And once again, I express utter bafflement at how anyone could look at recent human history and still hold the cheerfully optimistic opinion that "the advance goes forward to its intended goal."

Modern humanity loves to think of itself as a

Promethean, godlike maker of decisions and performer of socially redemptive acts of heroic goodness. God is not needed in a world where we are deciding, doing, acting, and changing everything for the better.

Of course, this is only an illusion, the vain hope of a despairing creature who feels that such illusions must be true or the presence of evil is unbearable. Illusions are long in dying, and they do not die until something changes our situation which enables us to forgo our fears, face facts, and live by truth.

On the whole, the theodicies we have surveyed in this chapter restored a more dynamic and cosmic perspective to the question of evil than the intensely individualized view of Augustine. They looked forward rather than backward, stressing the evolutionary quality of God's involvement with the world and a Lord who is forever "going before you" (Mark 16:7) rather than being locked into eternal retribution for some ancient wrong.

It is no great surprise that this type of theodicy has been popular in the last two centuries when the idea of social progress and the achievement of human betterment through political, economic, or technological means have been dominant.

But these theodicies were weakest in relation to our actual experience of ourselves and our history. Their justification of evil, sin, and suffering as necessary for human betterment failed to account for all the excessive hurt along the way. In the end, such theodicy must appear incredibly calloused to the one who suffers, incredibly naïve to the one who is confronted by the facts.

All life is an illusion. What then are the facts?

FIVE
THE LIMITS OF THEODICY

Rather than attempt to justify evil or to explain it away, perhaps we should be honest about its presence among us and then be honest about the limitations of God in eradicating this pestilence. If our theodicy is unwilling to blame evil on God, unwilling to see evil, suffering, and sin as somehow useful in achieving God's purposes, then why does God permit such pointless, threatening, painful realities to exist?

Meticulous Providence?

Some theologians would respond by challenging the notion of "meticulous providence." That is, they challenge the notion, implicit in much of our debate about evil, that God meticulously governs every event in life. Thus, Leslie Weatherhead begins his exploration of the will of God by saying, "We have got to get out of our heads the notion that everything that happens occurs because God wants it that way."

One reason that we call evil "evil" is that it is pointless, harmful, destructive, mischievous—no amount of theological gymnastics can make it otherwise. Therefore, rather than arguing that evil somehow fits into the purposes of God, let us simply admit that God is as upset

How can he draw that conclusion?

by the presence of evil as we are. God doesn't like it any better than we do, but God is unable to do very much about the situation.

Christians are not compelled to explain all occurrences of evil and to account for them in the divine scheme of things. Gratuitous, pointless evil exists in the world. A person who denies this is likely to deny or to distort actual experience. Thus, traditional theodicy, whether it be Augustinian, Irenaean, or developmental, ends up looking rather calloused by trying to construe every evil as necessary and justified. When we begin with the assumption that everything that happens occurs because God plans and directs it, we have a real problem on our hands and may be tempted to argue that evil is not really evil after all.

Thus, advocates of most traditional theodicies will argue that what we call "evil" is simply a result of our limited, provincial, time-bound way of looking at things. A child who is subjected to the surgeon's knife may feel that the pain is "evil" and utterly without justification. But the pain leads to greater, long-term good. We plan a Saturday picnic but must cancel it because of an unexpected storm. The storm is "evil" for us but, when seen as a whole, may bring good to farmers who grow our food.

Of course, the problem would be simple if the pain, evil, and injustice we suffer were like that of a successful surgical operation. But not everyone who sticks a knife into someone is a surgeon. Some operations, in spite of the pain suffered, lead only to greater pain. Storms not only bring bothersome showers; sometimes they blow down people's houses, kill, and destroy. We call much of the evil we experience "injustice" because it is simply that—unjustified.

Life has its tragic dimension. Anything we say about evil must still be able to admit to the tragic in life. Too much theodicy says, in effect, Isn't it nice that we are going to let God be God? We falsely idealize God and God's freedom, blaming everything on God, wondering why God would send such suffering. Then we devise elaborate theological and philosophical explanations to justify the ways of God to humanity. The end of all this is to be as magnanimous as possible in allowing God to be inscrutable and capricious.

But such thinking will not do. There is too much evil that doesn't fit into these tidy schemes. Recognizing the pointlessness, the injustice of evil, some contemporary Christian thinkers challenge the notion of meticulous providence. A popular example is the best-selling book *When Bad Things Happen to Good People*. The book has been a publishing phenomenon—over one million hardbacks and millions of paperbacks sold. In the book, Rabbi Joseph Kushner shares his thoughts on evil that arose out of his own family's struggle with a horrible illness. He rejects both the notion that suffering is a specific punishment which God brings upon us as a result of something bad that we have done and the popular idea that God sometimes sends bad things our way in order to test us or strengthen us.

Why do so many bad things happen to such good people? Kushner concludes that suffering exists because "even God has a hard time keeping chaos in check." God is the Creator, but a creator who has put the world together in such a way that accidents are bound to happen. The laws of nature work against us sometimes, and suffering is a part of life. When such things occur, God is outraged but also frustrated. God is doing his best, given the circumstances, but God is powerless to act.

No one could accuse Kushner of having an exaggerated concept of the power of God! As a primary example of divine powerlessness, Kushner uses the book of Job. Poor Job was the victim of some terribly bad events—loss of his family, loss of his possessions, a horrible sickness. For nearly forty long chapters, Job asks why. Finally, Job

67

receives an answer from God. God says (according to
Kushner), "Job, I'm truly sorry about what's happening.
It tears me up as much as it does you. But you know, of
course, that I had nothing to do with the way things
turned out. You know that I would love to help, but I
can't."

As Kushner says, "Bad things do happen to good people
in this world, but it is not God who wills it. God would like
people to get what they deserve in life, but He cannot
always arrange it. Forced to choose between a good God
who is not totally powerful, or a powerful God who is not
totally good, the author of the Book of Job chooses to
believe in God's goodness" (p. 43).

Kushner suggests that we should look upon evil as an
aspect of the uncompleted work of God, the chaos that
has not yet been overcome through divine creativity and
ordering. God may not like such disorder any better than
we do, but it represents "that aspect of reality which
stands independent of His will, and which angers and
saddens God even as it angers and saddens us" (p. 55).

While Job may have been gratified by God's candor and
empathy, we wonder if he was comforted in his suffering.
More important, as Philip Yancey says in a critique of
When Bad Things Happen to Good People, as bracing as
Kushner's picture of an honest but helpless God may be,
that is *not* what God said to Job. In one of the longest
speeches in the Bible, a speech that literally explodes
with striking images of the vast, wondrous, awe-filling
creation, Job hears God say:

> "Shall a faultfinder contend with the Almighty?
> He who argues with God, let him answer it." . . .
> Then the Lord answered Job out of the whirlwind:
> "Gird up your loins like a man;
>   I will question you, and you declare to me.
> Will you even put me in the wrong?
>   Will you condemn me that you may be justified?
> Have you an arm like God,
>   and can you thunder with a voice like his?" (Job 40:2,6-9)

Frederick Buechner says, "God doesn't explain. He explodes. He asks Job who he thinks he is anyway. He says that to try to explain the kind of things Job wants explained would be like trying to explain Einstein to a littleneck clam. . . . God doesn't reveal his grand design. He reveals himself."

In other words, what we hear in God's speech to Job is not impotence and kindhearted empathy, but rather the potent, all-embracing force of the God who made heaven and earth and all the creatures therein. If we are going to think about why bad things happen to good people, Job says that we must use terms that describe someone other than Kushner's kindhearted but essentially limited and impotent God.

So we come back to where we began this exploration of theodicy, the justification of the ways of God to humanity. We come back to Hume's challenge to the Christian faith: "Is He willing to prevent evil, but not able? then is He impotent. Is He able, but not willing? then is He malevolent. Is He both able and willing? whence then is evil?"

The central issue for believers is this: How can you believe the Good News when there's so much empirical evidence to contradict it? This, by the way, is the continuing question that our Jewish brothers and sisters keep raising before the church. If the Redeemer has come, why doesn't the world look more redeemed? If Jesus is also the Christ, how do you explain the Holocaust and a thousand lesser evils?

Thus the Jews represent, for Christians, our brothers and sisters in hope whose belief in God intensifies their experience of the world's unredeemed nature and challenges the illusions of the self-satisfied redeemed. As Jürgen Moltmann says in *The Church in the Power of the Spirit*, "Judaism impresses on Christianity the experience of the world's unredeemed nature." In so doing, these partners in hope are the "thorn in the church's side" because they constantly call us to give account of our hope in the face of the great evidence against it. This, Moltmann suggests, may be one reason for the church's history of persecution and hate of the Jews—they challenge easy claims of redemption to the core. The Jews challenge the church to hope, not on the basis of denial of the facts, but to hope by embracing the facts. Frightened by this challenge, we try to put the Jews away rather than confront them and the facts.

The Jews, by their very existence, remind all devisers of Christian theodicy that none of our philosophical explanations completely eliminate the rebuke of evil. Job's comforters and their smug, self-righteous, conventional explanations for his terrible plight are a warning to anyone who enters these intellectual waters. Their hardness of heart and blindness in arguing for God's justice destroy their ability to feel pity. They finally justify evil more than they justify God. This perhaps accounts for Rabbi Kushner's rather modest claims for God. No matter how great God may seem to us, no matter how good the work of God is, evil keeps seeping out somewhere. When all is said and done for our theodicies, a surplus of evil is always left over which no amount of philosophical explanation by contemporary comforters of latter-day Jobs can tidy up. Impressed by this, Kushner might agree with Woody Allen, who says at the end of one of his movies, "About the worst you can say about God is that he is an underachiever."

And yet Moltmann says that the church is also the thorn in the side of Israel as the church keeps trying to testify to the reconciliation of the world to God in Christ, without which there is no hope. Our hope must not be based upon denial or upon fantasies. It must be a real hope, an honest hope, a hope that dares to look the world and its evil straight in the eye and still is able to hope and believe.

Some theodicies expend too much effort speculating upon the causes of evil in the fall of humanity or of angels, or else they attempt to vindicate God's power and love. But the Christian need only "account for the hope that is in you" (I Peter 3:15). We are not called to "justify the ways of God to humanity." Rather, we are called upon to consider what the world and our lives look like in light of the Good News of Jesus Christ.

Christianity must be judged not on the basis of some ideal, some philosophical criterion for what is right and just, but rather on the basis of its truth. How effectively does it deal with good and evil as opposed to other competing responses such as apathy ("I don't really know because I don't want to take the effort"), fantasy ("I demand that God create a perfect world on the basis of my irrational standards of perfection"), nihilism ("The world is rotten, nothing is to be done about it, nothing should be done about it"), or suicidal despair?

The Christian faith steers a hazardous course between honest recognition of the suffering of the world and bold affirmation of the redemption of the world. This isn't easy. On the one hand, honesty can lead to defeatism. It may seem bracing to lift up Auschwitz as the supreme challenge to coldhearted theodicy. What comfort can we offer as evidence against such bleak, powerful, desolating evil? How callous of me to calmly reflect upon the death of Willie Earle and offer some reasoned philosophical response to such pointless, banal, bloody tragedy!

Such thinking simply hands the world over to the forces of darkness. Our noble admission of the work of evil in the world, in the absence of faith, is capitulation—complicity with the forces of evil without resistance or protest.

Along with our honesty about evil, we must somehow dare to recognize good. We must make the contrast between the two as vivid as possible, rather than say that evil is really good in the long run or helpful to the ultimate purposes of God. How odd that Christianity should be accused of being escapist when such faith is a

71

bold confrontation more powerful than pretensions of well-mannered, cynical despair or the endless equivocations of academic agnosticism! Hopefulness in the face of honest admission of the presence of evil is the human intellect's supreme challenge.

On the face of it, accepting life's darkness and malevolence as a truer picture of reality than life's goodness and benevolence may seem brave. But why exalt honesty in a world in which, if it is as empty and dark as some say, virtues such as honesty and bravery are meaningless? In that world, escapism is wisdom.

The Story as Our Starting Point

As attractive as Kushner's perspective on evil may be, it cannot be said to have arisen out of the biblical account of the nature of God. The Bible depicts Job not as the heroically honest questioner of the workings of God (as we enjoy thinking of ourselves), but rather as the man who in the midst of his questions met God, listened to God's questions, and thereby learned to ask his questions differently. The book of Job tells us how to think about evil, but Kushner fails to use that method in his own thinking about evil. Kushner thus derives a message about evil that does not correlate with the biblical story. To be a Christian, presumably, to be a Jew, is to be someone who demands that his or her philosophy of life correlates with the biblical story.

A Christian lives out the story of Jesus Christ. The story of the Nazarene who taught, healed, preached, suffered, died, and was raised is the criterion by which we view the world. It determines our point of view, our angle of vision, our perspective. The word *perspective* comes from the Latin, meaning "to see through." The story of Jesus gives us the view through which we see reality.

Christians differ from Hindus not because we are more honest than Hindus, certainly not because we are better people, but because we attend to differing stories. The Christian story is based upon and arises out of the Jewish story, but we differ from Jews because we read their story backward, as it were, reading back from the story of Jesus Christ. To be true to our faith means, in great part, being true to the story of Jesus.

Thus, questions are raised about the way I began this discussion of evil. As so often happens, I began thinking about evil with my story—my story of growing up in Greenville, in a world inhabited by taxi drivers and Willie Earle. Like many contemporary Christians, I tend to give a lot of weight to personal experience, my story, my feelings. I ask my story to explain the world for me, to tell me what is important, to raise the questions which then I go to Jesus to answer.

Traditional theodicy begins with our questions, our notions of what is good, right, and permissible, and then asks God why such bad things happen to such good people. Perhaps this is the primary reason why our theodicy has an untrue ring to it. It is all just a bit too tidy, too simple to cover the complexity of the experience. *My* story, as interesting as I may find it, is simply not complex enough to explain everything. Nor can I be honest enough in telling my story to truthfully confront reality. I need a story that enables me to be both honest and hopeful and that enables me to stare evil in the face without being annihilated by it.

Our account of evil must not resort to philosophical abstraction, because abstraction changes evil into something manageable and understandable which, whatever it is, is not evil. Our account must have the quality of a good story. A good story rings true. Life is not distinguished by easy solutions. Like a good story, life is tough, mysterious, and complex, full of subplots and diversions that do not seem to fit. All of our propositions must be in continual contact with true experience and with a coherent, truthful narrative which keeps judging the accuracy of our propositions. Unfortunately, in much theology, it works the other way around, with our abstract propositions telling the story of what is true, reasonable, and right.

The Christian claim is that the story of Jesus Christ, because it is true, is the one story that enables us to look at our lives and the world in a truthful way—to be honest and hopeful at the same time. We are to begin not with personal experience or autobiography but with the normative story which is Jesus Christ. Perhaps the story of Willie Earle points us toward the questions. But the biblical story rephrases these questions, configures them in a new way, and then moves us toward truthful answers.

No one has yet come to the Christian view of sin, evil, and redemption without being driven to it, not by philosophical speculation or by personal crisis, but by the crisis that is created in us when we are confronted by the Christ.

If Job learned anything in his long struggle with the question of evil, he did not learn it by delving into his own psyche or by having conversations with three smart friends. He learned when he came face-to-face with a God who speaks. Our wisdom comes the same way.

Curiously, the Bible is unconcerned with many questions that have occupied traditional theodicies. Contrary to Augustine, the Bible could care less where evil comes from; it only testifies that it is. Contrary to nearly all theodicy, the Bible doesn't engage in speculative analysis of what might have happened or what ought to happen. The Bible keeps closely tied to what is and what God reveals shall be. It discusses evil where we live, not before the beginning of time (Augustine) or after the end of time (Irenaeus and the developmentalists), but rather in time, leaving speculation to the philosophers.

So, having let my story—our story—raise some of the questions, having looked at some answers in various theodicies, let us turn back to the Story.

SIX

THE STORY

It is a strange story, the story of Jesus. It is not a biography, at least as we think of biographies, for the Gospels give us few biographical details. Matthew, Mark, Luke, and John evidently have some goal in mind other than the reporting of historical facts. Their goal is theological rather than biographical, pointing us to the Christ, the Annointed One, the Messiah who is Jesus of Nazareth.

He was born to a land long preparing for him, to a believing, hoping, suffering Chosen People who had suffered because of and in spite of their chosenness. Luke says that he was born into a poor family— an unmarried peasant girl and a humble carpenter. His nativity is painted against a dark background of Roman occupation, when "a decree went out from Caesar Augustus that all the world should be enrolled" (Luke 2:1). In spite of her pregnancy, Mary must travel to Bethlehem. There, in a stable, she gives birth to her son and calls him Jesus, Joshua, meaning "the Lord saves."

But what sort of salvation does this infant bring? His birth is proclaimed not to the high and mighty but to lowly shepherds "out in the field, keeping watch over their flock by night" (Luke 2:8). The religious leaders consort with the Roman military overlords to put an early end to any popular enthusiasm for this alleged "Messiah." King Herod orders that all male children be slaughtered. Mary, Joseph, and the infant Jesus flee to Egypt as political refugees until the persecution is over.

Soon out in the wilderness a harsh, new voice sounded. Repent! Prepare the way of the Lord! John the Baptist, a strange and abrasive prophet, called upon the nation to prepare, demanding that the people turn around, change their ways, and submit to a water bath as a sign of repentance and washing away of sin. To the complacent and religiously self-satisfied, John warns that "God is able from these stones to raise up children. to Abraham. . . . Every tree therefore which does not bear good fruit is cut down and thrown into the fire" (Matthew 3:9,10). One of these to heed John's call to baptism was Jesus.

Why should the Messiah be submitting to baptism? John wondered. In his baptism, Jesus shows the peculiar nature of his way of salvation, showing his solidarity with the people he has come to save. He will bring salvation, not by remaining aloof from and exalted by the people, but by entering into this life with them. His baptism is the beginning of that ministry of salvation.

What form will his ministry take? In the story of Jesus' temptations, Matthew gives us a glimpse of the dilemmas with which he wrestled. Dazzling alternatives were posed for him as he dwelt alone in the wilderness for forty days: command stones to become bread; throw yourself down from the pinnacle of the temple to be miraculously saved by angels; seize "all the kingdoms of the world and the glory of them." In other words, various tempting modes of salvation were proposed by Satan—gaining salvation through economic well-being, using divine power for spectacular exhibitionism, or seizing political power and setting things right the way the world does it (Matthew 4:1-11).

Jesus rejects these satanic temptations and returns to

his native Galilee to become the servant of God and humanity.

There, in his hometown, he announces that,

> The Spirit of the Lord is upon me,
> because he has anointed me to preach good news to the
>   poor.
> He has sent me to proclaim release to the captives
> and recovering of sight to the blind,
> to set at liberty those who are oppressed,
> to proclaim the acceptable year of the Lord.
>
>   (Luke 4:18-19)

To all who listen, Jesus announces, "The kingdom of heaven is at hand." That kingdom requires repentance as response to the judgment and wrath of God. But it also brings forgiveness and compassion. By his deeds of love, Jesus demonstrates the qualities of the kingdom. He casts out unclean spirits; he heals the troubled mind and the twisted limb. By his work, he shows that the coming kingdom means healing, liberation, and hope to all the oppressed. "If it is by the Spirit of God that I cast out demons, then the kingdom of God has come upon you," he says (Matthew 12:28).

And what a strange kingdom over which this Nazarene king would rule—strange when judged by our expectations of power and prestige. Here, insiders will be the ones whom the world treats as outsiders. "Blessed are the meek, for they shall inherit the earth," he says. "Blessed are the hungry, . . . the poor, . . . the persecuted." Those whom the world regards as the most lowly are called the most blessed.

"In this kingdom," Jesus says, "the last shall be first." When the religious leaders and scholars criticized him, he blisters them: "Tax collectors and harlots go into the kingdom of God before you" (Matthew 21:31).

He not only preaches the kingdom; he demonstrates it. He eats with despised "publicans and sinners." He refuses to condemn the woman caught in adultery, nor does he spurn Zacchaeus, a wealthy Jewish collaborator. To those who suffered from illness (which many thought came from their sin), he offered healing. To all, but especially to the "least of these" and the outcasts, he showed love—as great a love as the shepherd looking for one lost sheep, the father waiting for the returning prodigal son, the generous employer who pays the eleventh-hour worker as much as he pays those who have labored in the vineyard all day.

For everyone who heard him gladly, many more were deeply offended by this young prophet. John the Baptist spoke for many when he sent his followers to ask Jesus, "Are you he who is to come, or shall we look for another?" Jesus replied, "The blind receive their sight and the lame walk, lepers are cleansed . . . the dead are raised up. . . . And blessed is he who takes no offense at me" (Matthew 11:3, 5-6).

Yet many were offended. "By the prince of demons he casts out the demons," they sneered (Mark 3:22). His moral teachings turned conventional values upside down, as topsy-turvy a way of life as his kingdom itself. In his Sermon on the Mount, his gentle Beatitudes (Matthew 5) stand beside stern injunctions: "You have heard that it was said . . . 'You shall not kill.' . . . But I say to you that every one who is angry with his brother shall be liable to judgment; . . . whoever says 'You fool!' shall be liable to the hell of fire. . . . You have heard that it was said, 'An eye for an eye and a tooth for a tooth.' But I say to you, . . . if any one strikes you on the right cheek, turn to him the other also." Many, like the rich young ruler whom he told to "Go, sell what you have, and give to the poor," "went away sorrowful" rather than risk the cost of discipleship.

Controversy swirled around Jesus. If he were really the Messiah, why would he not let them crown him king and raise an army (John 6:15)? If he were really a prophet, why did he befriend sinners (Luke 7:36-50)?

Opposition to Jesus and his teaching intensified,

fanned by the hatred of religous and governmental leaders who feared both his message and his hold upon the common people. Even the folk in his own hometown rejected him. Jesus began to teach his followers that "the Son of man must suffer many things, and be rejected by the elders and the chief priests and the scribes, and be killed, and after three days rise again" (Mark 8:31).

But this was utterly unthinkable—that a Messiah should suffer and be rejected. It was beyond the reach of human imagination to conceive of a God who is willing to suffer and to serve, of a kingdom that is not established through coercion and violence.

At Passover, as pilgrims streamed into Jerusalem to commemorate Israel's deliverance from Egypt, Jesus and his disciples also entered the city. His procession soon became a multitude. He enters the city not on a war horse but on a donkey. He is greeted not by the mayor with the key to the city but by children waving palm branches and shouting, "Hosanna! Blessed is he who comes in the name of the Lord! Blessed is the kingdom of our father David that is coming! Hosanna in the highest!" (Mark 11:9-10). These "little ones," whom Jesus had called "the greatest in the kingdom," see their Savior.

But this Savior did not deal gently with those who had made a mockery of "my Father's house." The next day, he entered the temple and angrily drove the money-changers from their tables, cleansing the temple and demonstrating that his challenge was religious, not political or economic. Anger and resentment against him grew.

In the temple, Jesus healed the blind and the lame. He taught the multitude, criticizing those religious leaders who heaped burdens on the backs of the common people. He praised the meager offering of the poor widow and scorned the pretentious giving of the rich. "It is easier for a camel to go through the eye of a needle than for a rich man to enter the kingdom of God," he said (Matthew 19:24).

The arrest of Jesus came soon thereafter.

Knowing that the time was short, Jesus gathered for a meal with his disciples in an upper room of a home. The meal, which was celebrated in the context of Passover, would one day be seen by his followers as a foreshadowing of their liberation from death and sin, the beginning of a new exodus. When they gathered, Jesus "took bread, and blessed, and broke it, and gave it to them, and said, 'Take; this is my body.' And he took a cup, and . . . said to them, 'This is my blood' " (Mark 14:22-24).

Betrayers were present even among his disciples. "Behold the hand of him who betrays me is with me on the table," he said (Luke 22:21). Judas Iscariot was plotting to hand him over to the authorities. Yet, in the face of his disciples' betrayal and cowardice, Jesus prays for them in their temptations and even promises them an honored place in his kingdom. John's Gospel says that Jesus knelt down and washed their feet. "I am among you as one who serves," he says (Luke 22:27).

Shortly before dawn on that cold spring morning, a company of armed men arrived. At the signal from the traitor, Judas—a kiss, of all things—they arrested Jesus and led him away. His disciples, the ones who vowed to stand with him, come what may, forsook him and fled in fear into the darkness.

At a mock trial, Jesus was condemned for blasphemy and sentenced to death out of fear that he and his teaching would begin a riot among the people. Alas, those who once cried "Hosanna" when he entered the city now cried "Crucify him." He was condemned to death by crucifixion—one of the worst forms of torture ever devised by humanity—a slow, agonizing death which was reserved for slaves and the worst of non-Roman criminals.

Jesus went to this horrible, long, agonizing death with dignity, in spite of the taunts of his tormentors who stood at the foot of his cross shouting, "He saved others; let him save himself" (Luke 23:35).

He hung there in ignominy until he gasped, "Father, into thy hands I commit my spirit!" and breathed his last (Luke 23:46). Darkness covered the face of the earth.

It seemed to all that this was the last they would hear of Jesus of Nazareth. As the despondent disciples told the stranger on the road to Emmaus, "Jesus of Nazareth . . . was a prophet mighty in deed and word before God and all the people, . . . our chief priests and rulers delivered him up to be condemned to death, and crucified him. But we had hoped that he was the one to redeem Israel" (Luke 24:19-21).

"We had hoped. . . ." Now all hopes were dashed, crushed under the heel of the empire and the forces of darkness.

Then came an unexpected shout: *He is risen!* On Sunday morning after the Friday of the Crucifixion, some women came to the cemetery and found an empty tomb. Jesus had risen from the dead. "He appeared to Cephas [Peter], then to the twelve. Then he appeared to more than five hundred brethren at one time. . . . Then he appeared to James, then to all the apostles" (I Corinthians 15:5-7). Also "he was known to them in the breaking of bread" at the Emmaus meal (Luke 24:35). Something had happened that no one predicted, something beyond the bounds of human expectation and imagination— *Christ is risen!*

The once scattered, fearful, disillusioned, discredited followers were drawn together into a community—a community of the resurrection which joyfully proclaimed that, in Jesus the Christ, God had confronted the powers of evil, darkness, and death and had triumphed over all. In Jesus Christ, humanity had been liberated from all that enslaves it. His followers claimed not only that Jesus had been raised from the dead but that he was now present among them, bringing them from slavery to freedom, from death to life.

Now nothing could stop the Jesus movement. Nothing

could stop his followers from telling the story: Never again would the purposes of God seem utterly defeated. Never again would the forces of evil, oppression, and death seem so strong. The words thunder down through the ages, challenging all who hear them, "I am the resurrection and the life; he who believes in me, though he die, yet shall he live, and whoever lives and believes in me shall never die" (John 11:25-26).

The Story, Our Story

Being a Christian means to be part of a people who make the story of Jesus normative for the interpretation of their lives. But this does not mean that, to be a Christian, we must deny our own particular stories. For the story of Jesus means the Incarnation; that God Almighty has taken unto himself all of humanity, all of our history, stories, mortality, sin, suffering, and death.

The doctrine of the Incarnation is an affirmation that God enters into our humanity in such a way that our stories are reinterpreted, given meaning and hope because of the life and death of Christ. Christians believe that our story is a much better account of how the world works than are the stories the world tells. In this sense, the story of Jesus is crucial for us in a way that the story of my growing up in Greenville is not. In fact, if I am to understand my story, it shall only be through the vision of this man from Nazareth.

Jesus Christ is the key to the mystery of humanity. When the Son of God assumed human form, becoming a creature and calling God "Father," we learned that neither God nor humanity is alone; our destiny as sinful, frightened creatures has been inextricably bound to the love of God.

In Jesus Christ, God reveals the relationship between God and the world, a relationship with the One of whom it can be truthfully said,

> Surely he has borne our griefs
> and carried our sorrows;
> yet we esteemed him stricken,
> smitten by God, and afflicted.
> But he was wounded for our transgressions,
> he was bruised for our iniquities,
> upon him was the chastisement that made us whole,
> and with his stripes we are healed. (Isaiah 53:4-5)

Most theodicy doesn't work because it begins with ideals or abstract standards of what ought to be. It demands that God be "omnipotent" by our standards of power, "good" by our definitions of goodness. Invariably, the end result is not congruent with the story of the One who has "borne our griefs and carried our sorrows."

Who shall define *good* and *evil?* One reason why the world cannot stomach Christianity is that this faith has a peculiar, countercultural notion of what is good and what is bad. If I am a self-satisfied modern man or woman, *evil* might be defined as that which prohibits me from doing whatever I want to do—unfreedom.

While the Gospels do not provide formal definitions or concepts of good or, for that matter, evil—they give us particular glimpses of the good as an aspect of the kingdom of God. The good involves qualities that were explained to the disciples of John the Baptist—the blind see, the lame walk, the deaf hear, and the poor have good news preached to them (Luke 7:18-23, Matthew 11:4-5). Qualities which the world may regard as imprudent, idealistic, or weak—showing mercy, turning the other cheek, nonviolence, poverty, childlikeness—are called blessed.

How can it be, the world wonders, that an evil such as poverty, hunger, or persecution can be called blessed? In this world people who are poor are looked upon as failures, nobodies, the bottom of the barrel. Jesus calls them blessed because these Beatitudes arise out of a peculiar way of looking at the world, a kingdom vision based upon God's righteousness rather than upon human expediency.

We do this faith a great disservice when we claim that Christianity is reasonable or universally applicable. This faith is based not on universal standards of justice or human rights but rather upon the story of a Jew from Nazareth who lived briefly, died violently, and whom God raised. A Christian is someone whose values, whose ideas of good and evil are determined by this peculiar story which, for the Christian, is *the* Story.

Just as my being a Greenvillian, growing up in a world of Willie Earle and Tom Brown, determines my point of view, so my being a Christian, still growing up into the world of Jesus Christ, determines my point of view, enables me to discuss good and evil, *sub specie aeternitatis*.

A Christian and a Buddhist differ because they answer to different stories. The Buddhist, living under the story of the Enlightened One who trod the Eightfold Path to Nirvana, seeks to become disengaged from this world and its attendant evils. The Christian, following the crucified God, seeks to engage evil in the same spirit that Christ did.

The faithful affirmation that God's goodness cannot be defeated is a statement that cannot be made philosophically, logically, or experientially. It originates in the story of Jesus—in his willingness to give himself to death on Golgotha. If Jesus had died of a heart attack while lecturing his followers beside the Sea of Galilee, we would have a very different tale to tell. If there were no empty tomb, no promise and experience of the Risen Christ, we would have a very different idea about evil. As Christians we tell the story of Christ and repeat an ancient Latin motto, *Sic deus dilexit mundem*—"This is how God loves the world."

The astounding thing about the Christian story is not so much that there is a Christ, an Anointed One, a Messiah, a Savior. The amazing claim is that this Christ is Jesus, the Crucified One.

What are some of the implications for our exploration

of evil in this assertion that the story of Jesus is the story that makes all of our stories intelligible?

Sin

On the cross, human illusion and divine compassion meet. The cross challenges all notions that we are basically nice people who are making progress, that all we need is better education, better economic systems, better effort, and we shall be good. Jesus Christ was crucified by everything that people hold dear—religious ideals, governmental order, democracy in action, social revolution, biblical religion, tradition, national self-determination; they were all there at the foot of the cross as he bled and died.

So the story of Jesus reveals who we are even as it reveals who God is. We live in a fallen world that treats its saviors and its criminals in the same way, where the criminals are as likely to be those who wear black robes and sit in judgment as those upon whom we pass the sentence of death. The cross is God's *no* to humanity's aspirations and delusions.

Yet, the cross is also God's *yes* to humanity as God takes unto himself humanity's sin and rejection. Our awareness of our sin comes after hearing the story of Jesus, not before. We can only know the depth and seriousness of our sin when viewed through the perspective of the selfless love of Christ. Our sin is so serious, so deep-rooted in our thought and action, that we are as incapable of seeing it as a fish is incapable of noticing water.

We say that we act out of love—our "love" is but calculating egotism, an attempt to somehow subsume the interests of others into those of the self. We call our sin mistakes or ignorance, or justify it by the circumstances of our social background, economic condition, or some other factor that gets the blame off our back. Our confessions of sin are thus so much play acting, posturing, and other perverted attempts to look out for ourselves.

We can thus see why Luther claimed that it was a rare and difficult thing to become a sinner. Karl Barth was even more bold in saying that only Christians sin! Only Christians? "There is no knowledge of sin except in the light of Christ's cross," says Barth in *Dogmatics in Outline*.

Note that we usually try to deal with our sin through an opposite procedure. Most sermons within my ecclesiastical tradition begin with enumeration of all the evidence of human fallenness. After this list of sin has been given, Christ is brought forth as the answer to the problem.

Barth said that sin ought to be approached the other way around if we are to face our sin with seriousness. Barth's discussion of sin comes after his discussion of redemption. How strange that Christian theism should be as baffled by sin as it seems to be today, when Christian redemption may be the only way to admit honestly to the reality of sin. If this were not a story about God's willingness to take our sin and the tragedy of our evil unto himself, we would never be able to take it upon ourselves. We would be trapped in an endless web of romantic and idealistic delusions about our condition because we could do nothing more than look the other way.

The story of Jesus helps us to be honest about our stories, not to hide from or despise our humanity because God did not deem it an unworthy thing to become human. We need not lie about ourselves because the scriptural story is of a God who, even as he is hanging on a cross, says, "Father, forgive." Indeed, God's very nature is revealed as one who eats and drinks with sinners, who comes to seek and to save the lost. We need not hide from the gaze of this God. Nor must we hide our sinfulness from ourselves and others. Unlike the story of being a Greenvillian, which is often a story of the myth of racial harmony, a lie of innate goodness, a fantasy about a southern Eden, the story of Jesus provides me with the skills I need to be free from my self-imposed fears.

Real tragedy does happen in this life, as it did on Golgotha and on Highway 63 in Greenville. And the story of Jesus tells us that God is willing even to enter into real tragedy, to become tragic, in order to further divine purposes of adoption of humanity as beloved sons and daughters.

So the story of my being a Christian, someone who answers to a crucified God, enables me to claim the story of being a Greenvillian as my own. Because I am forgiven, I am able to see and to admit my story, just as it is. The fear of God is the beginning of wisdom. The worst thing he has said !. !

Augustine says in his *Confessions* that our life story seems like a chicken yard full of patternless tracks until, in the light of Jesus' redemption of us, we come to see that this meaningless maze, this mess, has actually been a story of constant forgiveness and persistent grace. We look back and see the hand of God tugging at our hearts until we were able to turn to God in love and thanksgiving. Our stories—even their worst, darkest, and most evil parts—are transformed into the means of our deliverance.

To encounter this story of Jesus is to be freed from the false stories that grip so many of our lives—stories of racial superiority, national innocence, human progress, the grand ideal. This story enables us to live without props or protection other than the truthfulness and love of God. And what a good story it is. Only a story this interesting—so cosmic, so daring, so real—could have the power to overcome our fatal self-absorption by directing our gaze to how marvelously the Lord of the universe is reaching out to us through the cross and resurrection of Jesus.

When all is said and done, my story has significance and interest to you only as an example of how even the tragedies and revelations in my life have been used by God to lead me to the truth which is Jesus Christ.

Redemption

Because the whole story of Jesus is normative for us, we must not only speak of the cross as a sign of human sin, we must also speak of the Resurrection. The resurrection of Christ, the surprise of the empty tomb of Easter, is the light that shows our evil for what it is—real, present, threatening but also defeated, impotent.

Two doctrines of the church represent the theologians' attempts to explicate the Story. The doctrine of the Incarnation speaks of the implications of "The Word became flesh and dwelt among us." The doctrine of the Atonement (actually, we should say doctrines, for there are many) says that, in Jesus, God has not only lived the human situation but has also changed it.

A rich array of metaphors describes the experience of atonement: victory (John 16:33), pardon (Luke 23:34), ransom (Matthew 20:28), service (Philippians 2:8), justification (Romans 4:25), sacrifice (John 1:29). All these images attempt to speak of the unspeakable surprise of a God who becomes flesh, then climbs a cross or sits at table with us sinners and says, "This is my body which is for you" (I Corinthians 11:24). For you. Broken for you.

A *Christian* view of evil begins here, in the story of atonement, and works its way backward to the roots of sin and evil and forward to the future triumph of God. For us, the problem of evil is not in its causation or origination, not even in its justification—contrary to the way in which evil is treated in most theodicy. The problem is how to work from our affirmation of redemption back to a clearer picture of our true condition as sinners who are redeemed, living in a fallen world which is being re-created.

In our honesty about evil, we must not concede too much. The Story doesn't allow us to be utterly pessimistic. God does not simply condemn evil or empathetically endure evil; God embraces evil, makes war with it, defeats it. God is not simply the victim of human sinfulness. God redeems our sin.

The Christian analysis of the human situation may seem pessimistic. Yet, Christians are among the few who dare to be honest about human sin because the Story teaches us to be optimistic about divine goodness. John Wesley claimed in a sermon that a bold assertion of human sinfulness was "the first grand distinguishing point between heathenism and Christianity." We usually think of Wesley's "going on to perfection" as an essentially optimistic view of humanity. However, Wesley's optimism was born of an honesty about human sinfulness that was derived from his blinding vision of the goodness and grace of God.

This is why Easter was the traditional high point of the church year—not Christmas, the feast of the Nativity; not Good Friday, the day of the cross; but Easter, the feast of redemption. All other liturgical seasons must be viewed from the perspective of Easter people who sing, "The kingdom of the world has become the kingdom of our Lord and of his Christ, and he shall reign for ever and ever" (Revelation 11:15b).

Our redemption must be more than a mere change of mind or heart, more than some new scheme for social engineering because we are powerless to change on our own. Redemption is an alteration in the structure of the world brought about by the work of Christ. Evil has been, is being, will be defeated.

Protestant Reformers such as Luther and Calvin were convinced, following Augustine, that sin is so deeply rooted in human thought and action that only a lifetime of conversion will root it out. The devil still howls. "No one is by nature Christian or righteous," said Luther, "but altogether sinful and wicked." Thus Nietzsche could sneer that bleak Christianity saw "man as something that must be overcome."

God creates something altogether sinful + wicked?

89

But the story of Jesus challenges a too pessimistic reading of the human condition. For one thing, the human race which we sometimes despise is also the people among whom our Savior chose to make his home. For another, Jesus Christ is Lord. "In the world you have tribulation," he says. Then, with a twinkle in his eye, "but be of good cheer, I have overcome the world" (John 16:33).

Any honesty about sin and evil begins by asserting the sovereignty of the God who enters the flesh, meets evil on its home turf, and defeats it. We start from the fact of our redemption, and then work from there back toward sin and evil. One must read the last chapter of this story first.

The triumph of the grace of God is the underlying melody underneath the various subplots and movements of the story of Jesus. The Christian knows something that the world does not, that "in Christ God was reconciling the world to himself" (II Corinthians 5:19).

Salvation is already accomplished. We cannot add to this accomplishment. All we can do, as Christians, is proclaim that it has happened. Consider these illustrations: The fire has been extinguished, though smoldering embers and smoke remain. However, a person in the upper story of the building does not know this and is under the illusion that the fire is still raging out of control in the floors below. He needs to be told that the danger has passed and that deliverance is at hand. His agony has no basis in reality.

Another illustration of the accomplishment of redemption: The enemy city has been captured and the government has capitulated. But the news has not yet reached all parts of the city, so minor sniping continues. The powers of darkness have been decisively defeated, but they have difficulty relinquishing their hold, even though they really have no more power.

A Christian is not someone who is better than other people. Rather, a Christian is someone who knows a story which others may not; namely, that the powers of death and evil, sin and rebellion have been decisively defeated. Our task is to proclaim that Good News, that Gospel, to all. The Christian life is not a way of procuring salvation; it is a way of attesting to salvation. The Christian is not someone who is working hard to bring about goodness; the Christian is someone who witnesses to the arrival of goodness in Christ and adjusts his or her life accordingly. We Christians gather in church, the community of the Resurrection, to tell the story, celebrate our deliverance, and lift up the symbols of our freedom. Because evil is still present among us, in defeated but nevertheless real forms, we must continually meet together in church to remind ourselves of what we so easily forget—Jesus Christ is Lord.

This astoundingly optimistic faith is based upon the conviction, which is itself based upon the Easter narrative, that Jesus is Victor. Here is God in human form, and no earthly or demonic power can withstand or defy the Living God. Here is a holy optimism which does not deny the reality of evil, yet which testifies that the forces of evil have been defeated through the victory of Christ.

When all is said and done regarding the presence of evil, we still have to account for the work of Christ on the cross. Was God in Christ reconciling the world to himself, making (in the words of the old service of Holy Communion) "a full, perfect and sufficient sacrifice for the sins of the whole world"? Before we dare speak of evil, we must stand as people who are confident of redemption. Then we can be honest.

The story of Jesus still unfolds, in your life and mine. Sin and evil may be defeated, but they lurk in our lives. So, in Christ, we continue to live out the story of his combat with the forces of darkness, "For he must reign until he has put all his enemies under his feet. The last enemy to be destroyed is death" (I Corinthians 15:25-26).

like doves + lambs?

What forces of darkness? 91

Why is death seen as enemy? Caterpiller consciousnes

We must continue to tell this story, distinguishing it from the world's other stories. We must continue to live as Easter people who know something that makes everything look different. We must continue to point to and to look for the movements of God in our time until that day when God is "everything to every one" (I Corinthians 15:28). In our struggles with evil, in our temptations and sin, even in our suffering and doubt, we are still able to lift up our heads and affirm with the Apostle that "we are more than conquerors through him who loved us" (Romans 8:37).

SEVEN
ADAM AND EVE

From the story of Jesus we move back to an older tale, one which, like my story, begins in a garden and ends elsewhere. It is preserved in the book of Genesis, the book of origins, told by a storyteller we have come to call the Yahwist. The Yahwist tells a story older than Israel, reaching back into the infancy of the human race, to Adam and Eve, Noah, Cain and Abel.

How did we get here?

The Lord plants a lush garden (Genesis 2:8). Here God places the man and the woman and plants "the tree of the knowledge of good and evil" as well as "the tree of life" (2:9). While they tend God's garden, man and woman are free to eat the fruit of all the trees with one exception: the tree of the knowledge of good and bad (2:16-17).

Why this tree? The "knowledge" here is experience—the opposite of innocence—rather than simply intellectual knowledge. The "knowledge of good and bad" is understanding, sophistication, complete wisdom which belongs only to God. As man and woman are told, when they eat of this forbidden fruit, when they aspire to be what they cannot, they shall die (2:17). Their arrogant lust for self-sufficiency and total knowledge shall be the source of their ultimate doom.

For now, man and woman "were both naked, and were not ashamed" (2:25). They were like children—innocent, unselfconscious in the idyllic garden.

> Now the serpent was more subtle than any other wild creature that the LORD God had made. He said to the woman, "Did God say, 'You shall not eat of any tree in the garden'?" And the woman said to the serpent, "We may eat of the fruit of the trees of the garden; but God said, 'You shall not eat of the fruit of the tree which is in the midst of the garden, neither shall you touch it, lest you die.' " But the serpent said to the woman, "You will not die. For God knows that when you eat of it your eyes will be opened, and you will be like God, knowing good and evil." So when the woman saw that the tree was good for food, and that it was a delight to the eyes, and that the tree was to be desired to make one wise, she took of its fruit and ate; and she also gave some to her husband, and he ate. Then the eyes of both were opened, and they knew that they were naked. (Genesis 3:1-7a)

Later commentators identified the serpent with the devil who brings evil into the world. (Recall how Augustine used the serpent to explain how evil appeared.) Such dualism is foreign to the Yahwist. The serpent is not a representative of evil (Satan), but a worker of ordinary mischief, a trickster, one who is crafty and cunning whereas the man and woman are innocent, immature, and susceptible to the serpent's tricks.

Note the psychological dynamics. First, the serpent caricatures God: "Are you sure that God told you not to eat from *any* of the garden's trees?" He reverses what God said in 2:16. The serpent assures the woman that, by eating the fruit, she will be like a god—she shall know everything.

But the woman herself saw that the fruit was "a delight to the eyes," a way to become wise. Humanity was not created in primordial innocence and perfection (contra Augustine). Man and woman are capable of contemplating rebellious actions. While the story does depict a "fall," the fall is the result of a "fallenness" which is innate. As Genesis 8:21 says, our thoughts were evil from the first. Despite all the later speculation upon the source of this fall and its reasons, the Yahwist seems uninterested in such matters. No need is felt to explain an undoubted fact of life which thousands of years of human history confirm: Humanity is defectible.

"She took . . . and ate; . . . and he ate." Contrary to centuries of misinterpretation, the woman is *not* depicted by the Yahwist as a seductive temptress who beguiles the man. This is not the Pandora's box myth by which the Greeks saw a woman's curiosity as the source of the world's evil. Male and female are equally rebellious.

The serpent's promise is fulfilled. The eyes of the man and woman are opened, but oh, how little they see! They expect to be as wise as gods, but all they see are their genitals. They know more than they did; namely, that they are weak, vulnerable, and naked. Their maturity is achieved, but Eden is lost in the process. With such worldly wisdom comes an infinite sense of sadness.

They make clothes to cover themselves. All culture, all human technological progress, is an attempt to cover our nakedness, so to speak, to hedge our vulnerability, our exposure to death. Unlike the animals, we are wise, we are *Homo sapiens*, which means that unlike other animals we know that we shall die. We are exposed. So we make clothes, write music, earn money, make swords, build bombs, design cities, and construct elaborate defenses to enfold us against the awesome truth that "you are dust, and to dust you shall return" (3:19*b*).

And they heard the sound of the Lord God walking in the garden in the cool of the day, and the man and his wife hid themselves from the presence of the Lord God. . . . But the Lord God called to the man, and said to him, "Where are you?" And he said, "I heard the sound of thee in the garden, and I was afraid, because I was naked; and I hid myself." He said, "Who told you that you were naked? Have you eaten of the tree of which I commanded you not to eat?" The man said, "The woman whom thou gavest to be with me, she gave me fruit of the tree, and I ate." . . . The woman said, "The serpent beguiled me, and I ate." The LORD God said to the serpent,

"Because you have done this,
    cursed are you above all cattle,
    and above all wild animals; . . ."
To the woman he said,
"I will greatly multiply your pain in childbearing;
    in pain you shall bring forth children,
yet your desire shall be for your husband,
    and he shall rule over you."
And to Adam he said,
". . . cursed is the ground because of you;
    in toil you shall eat of it all the days of your life;
thorns and thistles it shall bring forth to you. . . .
In the sweat of your face
    you shall eat bread
till you return to the ground,
    for out of it you were taken;
you are dust,
    and to dust you shall return."

. . . And the LORD God made for Adam and for his wife garments of skins, and clothed them. (Genesis 3:8a, 9-12, 13b-14a, 16, 17-19, 21)

The man and woman who once walked with God in the idyllic garden are now ashamed to be with God. When questioned, "Where are you?" the self-justification begins. Yes, the man admits, he did eat the forbidden fruit, but only because he was tempted by "woman whom thou gavest to me." By accusing the woman, the man insinuates the goodness of God to be the cause of his sin. Tragically, exegesis of this passage has often done the same, blaming woman for the fall of man. Man attempts to put the blame on one of God's beloved creatures. The woman, while a bit more straightforward, tries to blame another of God's creatures. First man blames the woman, who in turn blames the serpent in an attempt to ultimately lay the blame at the feet of God. What kind of God gives us these creatures who trip us up?

The serpent is not questioned. God's main concern is

the woman and the man. The serpent is merely condemned. Unlike most theodicy, the story shows little interest in the causes of wrongdoing. The Yahwist simply shows how quickly humanity was caught up in wrongdoing when given half a chance to do so.

After condemning the serpent's offspring to constant struggle with the woman's offspring, God turns to the woman not so much with a curse as with the dire consequences of human behavior. The pain of childbirth will be intensified. Childbirth was considered a great blessing, particularly to the Hebrews, a sharing in the creativity and fruitfulness of the Creator. Paradoxically, the blessing of God is now full of pain as a consequence of human sin.

The woman will want to have sex with man, even though it may lead to the great pain of childbirth; furthermore, she is destined not to possess the object of her urge but to be possessed by man. This is somewhat surprising, for the Yahwist no doubt participated in the male-dominated society of ancient Near Eastern culture. But it is precisely this male domination that is lifted up by the Yahwist as one more sign that creation is disordered and chaotic—so much so that the woman, who was created as a mutual companion for the man, is now under the subjugation of man. God didn't create it this way—subjugation of women is evidence of the chaos in human relations due to human sin.

When God turns to the man, there is a similar paradox. The good earth, from which man was made and which he cultivates, gives so little for his labors. Humanity is now at variance with its environment. The idea is not that work is punishment, for the Yahwist believes humanity was created to join in God's creativity, but that there is now conflict between man and the soil. The inhospitable dry and rocky soil of Palestine is a stark contrast to the idyllic life in the garden.

Here is life after Eden which the poet Henry Vaughan pictures:

> Things here were strange unto him: Swet, and till
>   All was a thorn, or weed,
> Nor did those last, but (like himself,) dyed still
>   As soon as they did Seed,
> They seem'd to quarrel with him; for the Act
>   That fel him, foyl'd them all,
> He drew the Curse upon the world, and Crackt
>   The whole frame with his fall.

Death is not an aspect of punishment. Immortality for humanity is not part of the Yahwist's vision. Death is simply the termination of our life of toil and conflict. "You are dust and to dust you shall return."

Yet the greatest paradox of all, the greatest source of conflict and struggle, is this: The knowledge that was supposed to make us like gods has only revealed to us our hapless finitude. We shall know the truth, the whole truth about who we are, and it shall make us—miserable.

Even amidst the stern rebuke to human presumption, the Lord God continues to care for the earthlings, rebellious creatures though they are. God makes garments to cover their nakedness as a sign of divine solicitude. Even in banishment, God continues to care.

Thus ends the somber story of humanity's first testing, its failure, and the consequences. "Therefore the Lord God sent him forth from the garden of Eden, to till the ground from which he was taken. He drove out the man; and at the east of the garden of Eden he placed the cherubim, and a flaming sword which turned every way, to guard the way to the tree of life" (Genesis 3:23-24).

Original Sin?

In contrast to the Pelagians, who taught that humanity was basically good and able to achieve salvation through an exercise of its own innate goodness, Augustine claimed that we humans are born into a world so sinful that, without some external redemption, we are without hope.

While we may or may not hold Augustine's view to be true (and I do), I cannot suppose that Genesis is an account of how this state of affairs came to be. The Yahwist, as we have seen, presupposes that humanity was capable of transgression from the beginning, even without outside assistance from the serpent. There was therefore no "fall" in the sense that men and women became something they were not; namely, sinful. Genesis 3–4 does not explain why humanity is alienated from God, why we are frustrated in our desire for immortality. Immortality is not something we forfeited by our sin but rather something that, in our sin, we failed to obtain.

We must take care not to read the thought of later theologians into Genesis. Augustine, for instance, developed the notion that sin is transmitted by sexual intercourse from parent to child in an unbroken succession going back to Adam. Augustine here relies on Paul in Romans 5:12 and upon Greek thought more than on the Yahwist. Indeed, I doubt that Paul had biological succession in mind in Romans 5:12.

The basic assumption of the doctrine of original sin is found in Genesis—the defectibility of humanity. But the traditional doctrine as formulated by Augustine is not. Paul's "inasmuch as all . . . sinned" (Romans 5:12 NEB) refers to the personal acts of all humanity rather than to the biological succession of a single sin committed by our ancestor Adam.

However, the doctrine of original sin does agree with Genesis that sin originates in human nature, by human desires and decisions. Our sin cannot be traced to some historical intrusion by Satan into our pure personalities, nor can it be blamed upon our social circumstances. It is a basic human disposition for which we ourselves are responsible.

The doctrine of original sin, first stated by Augustine in

fourth-century Africa, was reiterated by the Reformers in the sixteenth century. Sin originates with us. We are guilty for what we cannot help. No matter how idyllic our childhood, how superb our moral training and desire to be good, we invariably resemble Adam and Eve.

As Herbert Butterfield noted in his *Christianity and History*, the doctrine of original sin is the only empirically verifiable doctrine within the Christian faith. Many may doubt other Christian affirmations, but it is difficult to understand how they can doubt the evidence that humanity is defectible. As Kierkegaard said, "Sin presupposes itself" into all human endeavor.

You will recall that Augustine distinguished three kinds of evil—metaphysical, moral, and natural. Metaphysical evil is related to the fact of our finitude. Moral evil is evil that humans originate: vicious, perverse thoughts and deeds. Natural evil originates independent of human actions: bacilli, earthquakes, and droughts, including the suffering that inflicts the animal world.

For many thinkers today, natural evil rather than moral evil is considered the more damaging charge against God. Kushner's book *When Bad Things Happen to Good People* reverses the biblical assumption that the most perplexing issues involve us bad people doing bad things, all the time presuming that we are good folk of whom the worst that can be said is that we occasionally may do bad things. Unlike the Bible, we find the chaos of the natural world more disturbing than our own moral chaos. Unlike the Yahwist, we assume that natural evil precedes moral evil. The Yahwist indicates that the way to understand evil is first to look at ourselves before we charge nature with injustice. Sin is the root of evil.

A word of clarification is needed about this matter of sin. Many of us have grown accustomed to thinking of sin in criminal or legal terms. That is, sin arises only in those circumstances where (1) someone is confronted with two or more alternatives, and (2) one of those alternatives is known to be right and the other is known to be wrong. If the person then freely and knowingly chooses the wrong alternative, that person is guilty of sin. Our legal system does not hold people accountable if it can be shown that they were insane when they committed a crime. Only actual sin is punishable.

People who conceive of sin only as actual sin have absolutely no idea what to make of the traditional Christian notion of original sin. They believe that sin is episodic—an episode in a person's life when, for some inexplicable reason, that person made the wrong choice and selected the bad alternative.

But the doctrine of original sin is an affirmation that sin is thoroughly corporate and organic. Surely we have learned in this century that the most troubling, devastating aspect of sin is its corporate, systemic quality. In the church in which I grew up, we were taught to think of sin in purely personal, behavioral terms. Sin is sex, smoking, drinking. Of course, in a white, segregationist society, we dared not admit to the corporate nature of sin. Better to keep sin purely personal and individual.

Source of sin?

Has not this been a great weakness of American pietistic religion, to radically privatize and individualize sin rather than to acknowledge its corporate, institutional, systemic dimensions? The practice of beginning worship with a corporate prayer of confession arose in the Reformed tradition. Today, when such a prayer is used, people sometimes complain, "That's not *my* sin. My sins are different from someone else's sin. Why should I have to pray that?"

> Almighty and most merciful Father,
> we have erred and strayed from thy ways like lost sheep,
> we have followed too much the devices and desires of our
>   own hearts,
> we have offended against thy holy laws,
> we have left undone those things which we ought to have
>   done,
> and we have done those things which we ought not to have
>   done. (*Book of Common Prayer*, 1979 ed., pp. 62-63)

101

The rationale for a corporate prayer of confession is that our sin is corporate. Our problem is not so much what we do or don't do but rather the prior problem of who we are.

Is it fair for the Bible to say that the "sins of the fathers are visited upon the sons"? Whether it is fair or not, modern sociology and psychology document that it is true. The guilt of our forebears because of their treatment of the poor, the blacks, the native Americans is our guilt too. We all participate in, inherit, and are determined by these acts. Many of the advantages we enjoy today came as the result of our parents' injustice. We are in a tangled web of sin, much of which we had no part in but which determines the nature of our world. The Near East, Northern Ireland, racial tensions in the United States; we are guilty for what we cannot help. We pay for our parents' sins.

Why guilty? [margin note]

Sin is not only corporate; the doctrine of original sin states that sin is organic—one sin leads to another. We see this organic sin in the story of Adam and Eve. First there is the rebellion, then the lying, the blaming, the enmity, and on and on. Sin feeds on itself, has a life of its own once it is unleashed. Our sin infects our children, their children, the whole world. I look into the lives of my own children and, alas, their lives look like mine. Where to place the blame? Who first sinned here? Did the trouble in the Near East begin when American imperialism stepped in or when Israel invaded or when Syria attacked or when the first young man hurled a brick or when the angry refugee mother taught her children to hate? Sin reproduces itself.

Sin is not simply some act we commit now and then, not some momentary, episodic lapse in the human spirit: Sin is inherent in the human spirit. Sin is not a quantitative problem of adding up our alleged debits and credits; it is a qualitative problem of who we are rather than what we do.

Picture yourself at the beginning of your life—as a little

baby, an infant. Is this little baby, so cute and cuddly, a victim of original sin?

Yes, says the church. When the baby is hungry or uncomfortable, the baby cries out. Perhaps the child's parents are sleeping; perhaps they are occupied at the moment with some important business. This makes no difference to the screaming infant. The baby keeps screaming, keeps demanding attention, keeps insisting that the whole world stop and be attentive to his or her desires.

Of course, we know that crying is "only natural." It is essential for the infant's survival. And yet, is it not this self-centeredness that leads us to organize the whole world around ourselves? Is it not this egocentrism and self-concern that causes so much trouble throughout our lives? Isn't this our sin?

The picture of Adam and Eve in the garden is not only charming in its childlikeness; it is also accurate. Right at the first, in infancy, the trouble begins. As an infant I opened my eyes in the nursery in Greenville. Peering out from my crib, I saw the world around me. That is exactly how it appeared—around me. People came and went. All objects in the room were judged by my size, how they measured up to me, what they did for me. Those people or experiences that caused pleasure were enjoyed and I sought to duplicate them. I called them good. Those that caused me pain were avoided. I called them bad. My world, now larger and more complicated, long since removed from the nursery—from the garden, so to speak—is still securely fixed on its axis, still revolving around me. I am the measure of all things, the judge of all value, like a god unto myself.

Such is my sin, my original sin, originating in me. We have been at it since infancy, since Eden, and we will bring ourselves and everyone else to grief unless we can somehow be free.

Therein lies the human dilemma. We must be self-concerned in order to survive, but this egotism becomes the basis for all of our big and little acts of self-destruction. Was Paul overstating the case when he spoke of himself as "O miserable man"?

If natural evil is given primacy over moral evil, then it is tempting to see sin as mere privation (as Aquinas did), the unavoidable consequence of the feebleness of creatureliness. We thus see ourselves as objects to be pitied rather than condemned. Evil is rendered into a misfortune, a mistake in choosing what is good. This is exactly what happens in much contemporary social thought where evil is identified with ignorance or failure to realize one's potential due to misinformation or bad influences.

Plato, from whom Augustine's notion of evil as privation of the good was taken, could claim: "No man voluntarily pursues evil, or that which he thinks to be evil. To prefer evil to good is not in human nature; and when a man is compelled to choose one of the two evils, no one will choose the greater when he may have the less" ("Protagoras," in *The Dialogues of Plato*).

Plato was being overly optimistic. Of course people quite gleefully and willingly choose what is evil. Augustine argued, against the Platonic tradition, that evil is not simply a result of some deficiency in our nature but is a consequence of our corrupted will.

Sin is not merely privation. In the Bible sin is alienation, separation, misdirected will, rebellion. When the Bible speaks of sin, it does so in terms of lust, infidelity, fornication, and other sexual imagery in order to convey the personal, deep sense of our sin. Sin is adultery, the violation of God's fidelity with our infidelity. We must therefore beware of any attempt to speak of sin in an impersonal or abstract manner.

The Genesis story may not be literally or historically true; it is eternally true. The fall is happening today, in our own world, in Greenville. The story may not be an

Evil is relative

analysis of how our situation came to be; it is a picture of how our situation has always been.

There has never been some pre- or unfallen state, no matter how far back you go. We never existed in some ideal relationship with God, beginning in some paradisi- cal state and then falling into sin. All the characteristics that cause us pain and lead to rebellion, discontent, and suffering have been with us from infancy.

perhaps in spirit — before body

Any alleged "fall" took place neither when we ate of the forbidden fruit nor when we discovered our sexuality. It occurred when we lost our innocence, when we became conscious of our true condition, when humanity changed from being an ape into being *Homo sapiens*.

The story of Adam and Eve is a story about the difference between being an animal and being human. Human beings have eaten from the tree of the knowledge of good and evil. Unlike the animals, we find our lives complicated by conflicting values, moral questions, and the pain of having but not having immortality.

Sex is simple for the animals, a matter of being in heat or reacting to the rutting season. As the Yahwist notes, human sex is much more complicated—a source of creativity, yes, but also of much pain. Birth is easier for animals. A mother cat nurtures her young but then, in a short period, is done with them and fails even to recognize them a few months later. We humans, like all animals, must die. But only we know that we shall die. Herein is our "curse" and our nobility.

How do we know?

The idea of a "fall" still crops up from time to time in social thought. In the eighteenth century, Rousseau wrote that humanity had gradually fallen from a primitive state of original innocence into the current conflicts of classes, states, and individuals. Though Rousseau's Adam was not a Tarzanesque noble savage, natural man lived in a time when the conflicts of the ego were nicely balanced, before the tensions of civilization.

Rousseau's myth of a fall from a primal state of bliss continues today. In the back-to-nature countercultural movement of the 1960s, people sought to escape the tough social problems of the period by moving to rural communes. Marxists found the idea well suited to their purposes—modern economic systems, allied with the state, conspired to put the once happy workers in bondage, deprive them of their rightful labors, and give the fruits of their work to a new ruling elite. Marxists sought to reawaken in people a sense of their original state because, when people saw how happy they once were, they would rise up and throw off the chains of capitalist modernity. The *Communist Manifesto* stands as a touchingly romantic vision of a world before the "fall" which is to be restored through socialism.

The great disillusionment of our time is that such restoration has not happened, and it cannot happen because the idea of a "fall" from a state of original perfection is false. Most modern revolutions end in greater, rather than less, oppression of the masses. The Marxist nations of the world today stand as monuments to the worst sort of brutality and modern social engineering through military coercion. The people who tried to get back to nature found that nature is inhospitable when seen at close range.

What happened? The alleged fall from primal innocence and bliss never occurred. All the seeds of human evil and sin were present from the very first, as early as Adam and Eve, awaiting the advent of modern technology and governmental bureaucracy to exercise wickedness on a cosmic scale.

There never was a time when we existed as free human beings in some "state of nature" from which we subsequently fell into unfreedom. Our bondage has always been with us, within the very way we are put together as animals who know we shall die. (undergo transition).

Limitations and Abuses
of the Doctrine

Of course, a Marxist will respond that the doctrine of original sin has long been used to defend the social and political status quo. The church, we will be told, has conspired with economic and political oppressors to convince victims of oppression that they have no right to rebel because no one is innocent. Erich Fromm says that original sin favors authoritarianism.

While admitting to the establishment's abuse of the doctrine of original sin, I agree with Yale theologian George Lindbeck that the doctrines that have replaced it are far from improvements. Whereas conservative social thought often implied that the status of the downtrodden was deserved—they were lazy, immoral, heavy drinkers, so they deserved their poverty—at its best the doctrine of original sin contended that the privileged classes in no way deserved their status. They were not meritorious, merely fortunate. All have sinned, rich and poor, educated and uneducated, prince and pauper.

This equality in sin began to erode with Pelagian notions that human beings are not culpable and blameworthy, merely weak. The church had always distinguished between original sin—sin that is with us by our very nature—and actual sin, sinful actions that we commit as a result of our sinful state. The Pelagian view held sinfulness to be exclusively a matter of actual sin. Sin is what you do, not who you are. Because the upper classes were less likely to commit such actual sins as drunkenness, whoring, and idleness, many thought that they deserved their superior rank. This idea is in direct contradiction to Augustine and the Reformers, who consistently taught that sin is universal and that superior rank is mainly a matter of luck or inexplicable divine pleasure rather than merit.

Next, Marx and modern liberals simply overturned the meritocratic argument—the lower classes are deserving and the upper classes undeserving. Or they put forth a perverted Augustinian proposition that all are equally deserving rather than equally undeserving. Those who have less are automatically viewed as deprived of their rights, while those who have more are seen as the beneficiaries of ill-gotten gains. This is the source of the politics of resentment upon which socialism is based, even as capitalism has been based upon a politics of greed.

Whatever we might have against the traditional doctrine of original sin, we cannot accuse it of perpetuating unjust social arrangements by destroying the dignity of the oppressed by telling them that they are worse than their oppressors. Nor does it tell the oppressors that they deserve their good fortune. Rather, the classical doctrine told the privileged that their privileges were wholly undeserved and ought to be used for the common good. It also paved the way for future revolution and social change by saying, as we saw in the story of Adam and Eve, that current social arrangements are the chaotic result of original sin. As Lindbeck notes, what the doctrine could not do was authorize active struggle against an unjust establishment, and that was its fatal flaw.

The American theologian Reinhold Niebuhr attempted to affirm the doctrine of original sin as empirically right and biblically accurate while correcting some of its weaknesses. Niebuhr argued that, while we ourselves may not be oppressed, biblical faith compels us to take up the cause of the oppressed as if it were our own. We must wed the concept of sin to the concept of divine justice. Original sin says that the human race is not perfectible and is responsible for its imperfections. There will be no capitalist, Marxist, or socialist utopias before the Second Coming and yet, as Christians, we are compelled to join with God in working for justice and living in the light of the coming kingdom of God which Jesus announced and initiated by word and deed. War, injustice, sexism, racism, and violence will not be eliminated. Every advance in human welfare brings new perils, for our best efforts are still corrupt. No saints are without sin. Yet we must work with God by sharing in divine creativity and works of goodness and by opposing injustice, not for ourselves, but for our neighbors.

Niebuhr believed that only in those societies where the Christian concept of original sin flourished could democracy develop, because only a society with a healthy respect for the corruptibility of individuals and societies would fashion democratic systems of checks, balances, and competing rights. In *The Children of Light and the Children of Darkness*, Niebuhr states: "Man's capacity for justice makes democracy possible; but man's inclination to injustice makes democracy necessary."

To be a Christian who engages in politics and who still believes in the doctrine of original sin is always to maintain a healthy skepticism of the polarized enthusiasms of the Right or the Left and to be highly distrustful of the self-righteous crusading spirit—especially distrustful when this crusading ardor has no ability for self-criticism, especially when it is tempted to caricature its foes as evil and its friends as wholly righteous. In contemporary America, in the world at large, to be a believer in the doctrine of original sin is to feel quite lonely while standing upon this increasingly deserted middle ground.

The devastating human sins of self-righteousness and holy arrogance infect the Left no less than the Right, the peace movement as well as the military-industrial establishment, liberation theology in addition to its critics. Reformers, no less than reactionaries, do not like to be told that maybe—just maybe—they may be wrong, that their reforming zeal may be infected by a host of impure motives.

But those who would remind reformers and reactionaries of sin must begin by being conscious of sin within themselves. It is all too easy to sit back in aloof contentedness and point to the sins of others, but this is surely the most dangerous sinfulness of all. As Lindbeck says,

> We need to guard against the leftist illusion that because structures need changing, a prior change of heart is unimportant; and the rightist supposition that because hearts need changing, social and political action is pointless. . . . Perhaps only when our hearts are changed so that we apply the doctrine of original sin to ourselves, will we be able to make a specifically Christian contribution to the struggles against injustice, poverty, war, racism, sexism and the destruction of the earth's ecological balance. ("Politics and Original Sin: The Uses and Abuses of a Doctrine," *Reflection*, April 1983)

The idea that sin originates in us and is always with us, from infancy, from Eden, and that it is something deep, primal, and unavoidable in all human thought and action may be the specifically Christian point of view that we have to offer to contemporary political discussions.

Pooh!

Sighing for Eden

It may seem cruel that the Creator has made us as creatures who grow old, suffer, and die and who, because we are wise enough to be conscious of our finitude, are also prone to improper self-interest and sin.

In the garden, humanity is not some angelic being dwelling in primal perfection, but a frail, uncertain creature living in a world both friendly and hostile, a world created by God but also in which God is only an occasional visitor.

We cannot identify the serpent in the garden with later ideas of Satan, but we should mention Satan before leaving this stage of our investigation.

Where did evil come from? One traditional theory for the genesis of evil has been that evil was introduced by

Satan, a fallen angel. Satan, so the reasoning goes, was originally good, but he rebelled against God and is now bad. Thus God has no responsibility for the presence of evil and sin. I do not find that the notion of Satan, an evil being in opposition to God, advances our understanding greatly.

I agree with the Yahwist that the whole mystery of sin lies in *my* perversity, a mystery which reference to diabolic beings does nothing to clarify. Interestingly, Augustine used Satan in an attempt to exculpate God. We now use Satan to exculpate ourselves—the devil made me do it. Yet, when all is said and done, the doctrine that sin originates wholly within ourselves is one of the most significant things we can say about humanity—it makes us responsible.

Our understanding of evil is not advanced by removing the discussion to a superhuman plane. To do so is to risk scapegoating—isolating evil, making it specific and separate. Hitler did this with the Jews. The demonic is subhuman, nonhuman. What are we to do with it? We liquidate, exterminate, re-educate, relocate. Then we label some political or economic structures as evil. Goodness is the opposite. God is on the side of the poor. The rich are demons. Our political opponents are incarnations of the demonic. In so doing, we forfeit the ability to look critically at our own strategies and programs. We have met the enemy, but the enemy is not Satan. The enemy is ourselves. Evil wears a human face.

People continue to believe in Satan because temptation does feel personally seductive. We are mystified by the ease with which we succumb to perversity, by how often evil masquerades as good, by how many of our best-intended actions stem from unconscious, evil motives. But we need look no further than our own hearts.

There is only one God in the world, only one Lord. This God has no rivals. We face God directly, without the need to worry about the work of evil intermediaries. Our sin is our problem. We ourselves are the only source; God the only answer.

In *King Lear*, the scoundrel Edmund admits that his vile nature cannot be blamed on something outside himself. He ridicules those who look to Satan or the stars or some other force as the origin of wickedness:

> This is the excellent foppery of the world, that, when we are sick in fortune,—often the surfeit of our own behavior,—we make guilty of our disasters the sun, the moon, and the stars: as if we were villains by necessity; fools by heavenly compulsion; knaves, thieves, and treachers, by spherical predominance; drunkards, liars, and adulterers, by an enforced obedience of planetary influence; and all that we are evil in, by a divine thrusting on: an admirable evasion of whoremaster man, to lay his goatish disposition to the charge of a star! My father compounded with my mother under the dragon's tail; and my nativity was under Ursa major; so that it follows, I am rough and lecherous. Tut, I should have been that I am, had the maidenliest star in the firmament twinkled on my bastardizing. (*King Lear*, Act I, scene 2)

Evil is not some external intrusion into human existence; it is the result of freedom misused, our improper response to our finitude. As Niebuhr says, we are like a sailor who climbs the mast, with the abyss of the sea below, the glory of heaven above, finding himself full of anxiety over how high he may climb or how far he may fall. We are animals, yet we are created in the image of God. We sigh for Eden, for that world which was but never really was. Ironically, out of our sighing, our desperate longing to be good, our anxiety to know everything and to live forever, comes our sin.

EIGHT

CAIN AND ABEL

As Genesis tells it, it didn't take long for things to go from bad to even worse. In this chapter we turn our attention to another strange, old story. Here is the true age-old story of human resentment, hate, violence, death, fear, blessing. It is the story of Cain and Abel.

At dawn, in the early morning of humanity, a woman cries out, "I have gotten a man with the help of the LORD." Eve's is the jubilant cry of a woman who finds herself sharing in God's creativity. But it is also a bit of the same old arrogance that led to eating the forbidden fruit. The Lord made the first human being; now she too has produced a man.

Now Adam knew Eve his wife, and she conceived and bore Cain, saying, "I have gotten a man with the help of the LORD." And again, she bore his brother Abel. Now Abel was a keeper of sheep, and Cain a tiller of the ground. In the course of time Cain brought to the LORD an offering of the fruit of the ground, and Abel brought of the firstlings of his flock and of their fat portions. And the LORD had regard for Abel and his offering, but for Cain and his offering he had no regard. So Cain was very angry, and his countenance fell. The LORD said to Cain, "Why are you angry, and why has your countenance fallen? If you do well, will you not be accepted? And if you do not do well, sin is couching at

See "Good News" in [ ].   113

the door; its desire is for you, but you must master it."
Cain said to Abel his brother, "Let us go out to the field."
And when they were in the field, Cain rose up against his
brother Abel, and killed him. Then the LORD said to Cain,
"Where is Abel your brother?" He said, "I do not know;
am I my brother's keeper?" And the LORD said, "What have
you done? The voice of your brother's blood is crying to
me from the ground. And now you are cursed from the
ground, which has opened its mouth to receive your
brother's blood from your hand. When you till the ground,
it shall no longer yield to you its strength; you shall be a
fugitive and a wanderer on the earth." Cain said to the
LORD, "My punishment is greater than I can bear. Behold,
thou hast driven me this day away from the ground; and
from thy face I shall be hidden; and I shall be a fugitive
and a wanderer on the earth, and whoever finds me will
slay me." Then the LORD said to him, "Not so! If any one
slays Cain, vengeance shall be taken on him sevenfold."
And the LORD put a mark on Cain, lest any who came upon
him should kill him. Then Cain went away from the
presence of the LORD and dwelt in the land of Nod, east of
Eden. (Genesis 4:1-16)

Just as the story of Adam and Eve speaks of temptation
and a "fall," so does the story of Cain and Abel, though the
crime here is fratricide rather than unlawful acquisition
of esoteric knowledge. Both stories end in banishment.
The Yahwist uses the story to illustrate further that the
first rebellion against God quickly leads to another.
Humanity will not respect the limits set upon its
existence.

Adam and Eve have a son—Cain, firstborn of the
human race, great-great-great-granddaddy of everyone.
Cain.

And then a second son, Abel, is born, and clouds gather.
Second son. Psychologists say that the birth of another
child is one of the most traumatic, psychologically
determinative experiences a child can have.

"Mommy, she's nice, but let's take her back to the
hospital now," said our firstborn barely four hours after
his new sister had been brought home. He knew!

So this is a story about Cain—firstborn, and Abel—little brother, interloper. My friend John Bergland says that out in frontier Montana, when his missionary father preached this story to a group of rough sheepherders, you know whom they were cheering for!

It seemed only right to them that God found Abel's sacrifice "acceptable." And when they heard of Cain's anger, all asked with one voice, "Can Abel be blamed that God finds his mutton more 'acceptable' than Cain's vegetables?" And when they were told that Cain killed Abel every sheepherder in the house went for his gun—"Those blasted farmers," they cried, "with their fences and homesteads and plows; we were here first."

Who is the hero of this story? Surely it cannot be the farmer Cain, the murderer. Then it must be the shepherd, Abel. He must have done something that made him God's fair-haired child.

But the story does not say why Abel's sacrifice was more acceptable than Cain's. In fact, when Cain complains that God has shown favoritism to Abel, God seems shocked that Cain is upset: "Why are you angry, and why has your countenance fallen? If you do well, will you not be accepted? And if you do not do well, sin is couching at the door; its desire is for you, but you must master it" (Genesis 4:6-7).

The story does not say that God loved one and not the other. It simply says that God "had regard" for the offering of one. Thus, it is a story about God's inscrutability which overshadows our moral ideas of right and wrong, good and bad. Genesis is full of these inscrutable divine choices: Abel over Cain, Abraham over his brothers, Isaac over Ishmael, Jacob over Esau. When we think about good and bad, sin and evil, there is always this cloud of unknowing because we are human and not God.

Not long ago, I read this story to my children during our family's Bible story time at breakfast. The storybook said, "Why did God accept Abel's offering but not

SIGHING FOR EDEN

Cain's? Because Abel offered his sacrifice in the right spirit."

That may seem reasonable to us, but that is not the story. God is surprised that one of the boys is hurt by the choice, as surprised as any loving parent who is asked by a child, "Why do you love Susie better than me?"

A parent finds the question surprising because Mama and Daddy love both children. So God asks Cain, "Where is Abel your brother?" Your *brother*. And isn't that just the problem? The problem is that God is my brother's God too! Cain's problem—my problem—is not that I am not loved, but that God does not love only me.

When questioned about his crime, Cain does not merely reply evasively as did his parents, Adam and Eve; rather, he counters God's interrogation with an outright lie. To this he adds an insolent and sarcastic retort, "Am I my brother's keeper?"

The problem is not that God accepts little brother and does not accept me; the problem for Cain and for me is the human problem that God accepts both me and little brother. It is deeply discomforting to hear Paul affirm that with God "there is no distinction" (Romans 3:22) or to hear Jesus note that "he makes his sun rise on the evil and on the good, and sends rain on the just and on the unjust" (Matthew 5:45). It is not easy to love a Messiah who is a friend of tax collectors and sinners, who sees bad ones going into the kingdom before us believing, tithing, good ones. And when God's love comes through to me so impartially, so unexceptionally, I begin to hate little brother and wish he were dead so that I could have God all to myself. Such is the origin of most human hate.

Davie Napier hears Cain mutter to himself:

I hate his guts, I hate the guts of Abel.
I'm sick of Abel, sick to death of Abel.
Sick of brother sick of Fellows
Blacks and Reds and Browns and Yellows
sick of each minority

116

pressing for autonomy
sick of white men ugly white men
arrogant and always right men
sick of sick men sick of sickness
Protestant- and Catholic-ness
sick of every lying bromide
Happy Birthday Merry Yuletide
freedom truth and brotherhood
Reader's Digest motherhood
pledge allegiance to the flag
"under God"—now what's the gag?

Sick of vicious ostentation
sick of humor's constipation
sick of sickness human sickness
human greed and human thickness.

Get my brother off my back
White Red Yellow Brown and Black.
Perish Abel perish quick—
One of us is awful sick.

Scapegoating is the inevitable result of our failing to admit to the evil within our own murderous egotism. Refusing to take our evil seriously, we pin it on others. There is no other way for the incurably optimistic to explain the presence of evil deeds except to see the Soviets as "animals," Jews as "money grabbing," blacks as "lazy." Why is our economy a mess? Round up illegal aliens, smash Japanese autos, get the secular humanists out of the schools and the Jews out of the banks.

Sin is "couching at the door"—and always has been. Like some demon, it waits for the right moment when I am weakened by resentment. *Homo homini lupus,* "man is a wolf to man," is a saying which may be unfair to wolves, for only humanity consistently kills its own species.

I see myself as the victimized, persecuted little brother Abel. It's not my fault that God loves me more than big brother Cain. It's not our fault that we live in the world's richest, most powerful nation. Such things are only right considering all the good things we have done for God.

Alas, I am Cain; my hands too have blood on them; the earth cries out at my sin. When I look back upon my story, I see Willie Earle; Tom Brown; the poor, both black and white; Iranians; native Americans; brothers and sisters near and far whom I see not as kin but as enemies, competitors in my lust to be God's only begotten son. This is a story about me.

Recently, a young man told me about an incident that happened to him while he was riding his bike down a mountain road above Greenville. He heard a car approaching behind him at a high rate of speed. He looked behind just in time to see the car veer toward him, forcing him off the road and into a ditch. The car slowed but did not stop. He was surprised, he said, about what happened.

"It is surprising and disturbing that people would do something like that," I said.

"No, that wasn't what surprised me," he continued. "I was surprised that the minute I hit the ground, I frantically searched for a rock, a pipe, anything. If that car had stopped, I would have taken that rock and bashed the brains out of the guy who tried to do that to me."

I assured him that his anger was quite understandable.

"But I am a college graduate," he said.

How hard to believe that we are Cain. The point of these little Bible stories is never, "Oh, if we could only be like the wonderful saints of the Bible." The point is, "God help us, we already are like them."

It is tempting to look for the evil one and then point with indignant moral conviction at him or her, to caricature evildoers as demonic, satanic, crazed maniacs. Whenever television dramatizes Hitler, I have noted he is always presented as a brooding, maniacal, crazy man. Who would have been foolish enough to follow such a devil? The real Hitler, according to his contemporaries, could be quite charming, even endearing. He neither smoked tobacco nor used alcohol. All Hitler wanted for Germany was peace, justice, and national self-determination.

Of course, we caricature the Hitlers, Stalins, and Pol Pots of the world because we so desperately want to believe that we are not like them.

In *The Gulag Archipelago*, Solzhenitsyn says: "If only there were evil people somewhere insidiously committing evil deeds, and it were necessary only to separate them from the rest of us and destroy them. But the line dividing good and evil cuts through the heart of every human being."

The thing that prevents us from being Attila the Hun is lack of chance. Any evil we come upon in the clenched fist of Cain has already been encountered in our own inclinations. As Jesus noted, there's not too much distance between the actual adulterer and all those of us who regularly commit "lust of the heart." Anyone who looks upon his or her little brother and sneers "thou fool" (and who among us never has?) should feel kinship with the person on death row who awaits the noose.

Cain is not the hero of this sordid and bloody story. Nor are you and I heroes here, for we know that we are no better, no worse, than Cain. Nor is even the victim Abel the hero. The hero of this story is God.

From the dim, dark, early days of our history, says Genesis, we want to do right. We want to love and to be loved. But from the very first, the first great-great-granddaddy of us all—God help us, we can't. "Sin is couching at the door"—our resentment, pride, selfishness, destructive, self-securing lust. God help us; we can't help ourselves. God help us.

Curse and Blessing

Cain is humanity under a curse, those against whom the whole creation has a grudge. Even in nature, we are homeless and at war. Cain is sent into exile for the

Outgrowing?

Perhaps thoughts are as important to God as deeds.

murder, condemned to wander east of Eden in the lonely, shadowy "land of Nod" (which means "wandering"). The "fall" in Eden has continuing social consequences; it is not restricted to some private and personal offense against God but rather leads to offense against the whole human race and results in the long tragedy which is human history.

"My punishment is greater than I can bear," says Cain. (It is always God's fault in these matters.) "Behold, thou hast driven me this day away from the ground; and from thy face I shall be hidden; and I shall be a fugitive and a wanderer on the earth, and whoever finds me will slay me." Abandoned, exiled from civilization, the murderer is cast out, away from the divine plan, punished.

Well might the story end. And we would judge it to be at least an accurate story, though not a particularly pretty one. It is a story of our ancient resentment, hate, violence, death, fear, and alienation. We have heard it all before and, alas, we shall surely hear it again.

The curse is therefore quite believable, understandable. We get our just deserts in the land of Nod. But, when the judge speaks, the word, surprisingly, is a word of mercy which contradicts Cain's fear. "Not so!" says God. The Lord will work vengeance on anyone who touches Cain. The Lord still has plans, even for the murderer Cain. The Lord puts a mark on Cain, a mark not of punishment but—surprise—a mark of blessing.

Murderer that he is, Cain is marked, set apart, sealed by God. Cain, who deserves to get clobbered for his sin, gets clobbered with grace. God gets the last word in—a word of grace. Vengeance belongs to God (Psalm 94:1); so does mercy. For some inscrutable divine reason, this murderer is still precious to God.

This is not the same old sad story of our sin, selfishness, violence, and death. It is a surprising story of God's grace. We must read our stories in the light of God's story. It is a story about God's amazing willingness to take our

120

humanity; our frailty; our murdering, tooth-claw-and-nail cruelty; our limitations, and weave them into his purposes. Again and again, the Bible says, God's grace isn't stumped by our limitations.

Israel asked, "Why did God deliver us and bring us to this good, green land of milk and honey? It must have been because we were so good, so sinless and holy a people that we naturally deserved such blessing."

No, says the Yahwist. No, you deserved not blessing but a curse. Your great-great-granddaddy was the murderer Cain. You are here by grace.

The same God who loved little brother Abel, wonder of wonders, finds a place in his great heart even for big brother Cain. This God shall preserve Cain, make something out of him, a Chosen People. The one who deserves death is given the sentence of life. In spite of the blood on his hands, Cain finds that he does not have to be a good little boy with clean hands to be chosen by God. You don't have to be a good little nation with a clean slate and an inspiring history to get chosen.

And so Paul could say to that dirty-handed crowd at First Church Rome:

> But now the righteousness of God has been manifested apart from the law, although the law and the prophets bear witness to it, the righteousness of God through faith in Jesus Christ for all who believe. For there is no distinction; since all have sinned and fall short of the glory of God, they are justified by his grace as a gift, through the redemption which is in Christ Jesus, whom God put forward as an expiation by his blood, to be received by faith. This was to show God's righteousness, because in his divine forbearance he had passed over former sins.
> (Romans 3:21-25)

The Bible is not a story of saints and their great commitment and courage to serve God. The Bible is mostly a story about God's great commitment and courage to serve sinners like us. No evil that we or our great-great-grandparents commit is beyond God's power to redeem. Time and again when he has come to love us, we have hung his beloved ones on some cross, only to have him turn that cross into a sign of blessing.

Time and again in our story, even out here in the land of Nod where we wander, out here east of Eden, with the blood of little brothers and sisters still sticky on our hands and the whole creation set against us, this One has come to bless us, to mark us, to choose us so that his grace might make something out of us, even us, in spite of us.

For now, Cain must learn to live with God's absence, as an exile. Cain's descendants shall found cities and build towers, shall sing songs and make music and develop the art of forging, discovering the sword and adopting it as the approved instrument for human disputes. In the next story (Genesis 4:17-24), Lamech wildly celebrates the glories of boundless human revenge and the power of the sword. Now Cain's people have the bomb, so with an efficiency unknown to Lamech, we can avenge seventy million times seven. The sorry story goes on and on.

No doubt Cain longs to return to Eden. But he cannot go back. He does not know what the future holds. He is therefore left with only the protective absence of God, safe for now but displaced from Eden: an exile. He is a lonely and troubled wanderer, yes, but an exile for whom God has something in mind.

Basic messages of story:
1) The ritual of sacrifice is pleasing to God.
2) God can be vengeful.
3) God loves us, no matter what. (Loves Cain as much as Abel, Hitler as much as me.)

NINE

DAVID AND BATHSHEBA

Man produces evil as a bee makes honey," said the English novelist William Golding. "I do not understand my own actions," confessed Paul. "For I do not do what I want, but I do the very thing I hate. . . . So then it is no longer I that do it, but sin which dwells within me. . . . I can will what is right, but I cannot do it. For I do not do the good I want, but the evil I do not want is what I do. For if I do what I do not want, it is no longer I that do it, but sin which dwells within me" (Romans 7:15, 17, 18b-20).

Whatever Became of Sin?

In the church, we once talked a great deal about sin. For us, sin was forever "couching at the door." To "live in sin," much less to "die in sin," was a great tragedy. People seem not to be troubled by sin today. Our sermons are preoccupied with idealistic, even romantic talk of liberation, caring, community, and programs to develop our essential goodness. Over the years, Christian theology has fallen into step with the march of secularism. The transcendent dimension of life has been rationalized and desacralized, eliminating sin, for sin is, by definition, violation of the sacred. While Augustine's linkage of sex and sin had unfortunate consequences, it at least

123

affirmed that sex is a mysterious, value-laden endeavor where people get hurt and sometimes destroyed. Now sex is desacralized recreation with little at stake beyond the momentary satisfaction of the participants. Sex has become a neutral, value-free endeavor, a matter of lifestyle options—not sin. For something to be sin, sacredness must be violated.

In his popular *Whatever Became of Sin?*, Karl Menninger chronicles the demise of sin sometime around the turn of the century when science advanced the view that masturbation was not really as bad as was once thought:

> A taboo thousands of years old vanished almost overnight! Masturbation, the solitary vice, the *sin* of youth, suddenly seemed not to be so sinful, perhaps not sinful at all; . . . less a vice than a pleasurable experience, and a normal and healthy one! This sudden metamorphosis in an almost universal attitude is more significant of the changed temper, philosophy, and morality of the twentieth century than any other phenomenon that comes to mind. It is not difficult to see why *all* sin other than "crime" seemed to have disappeared with this one.

Why this particular sin? Because, says Menninger, in the minds of ordinary people, sin was linked to the misuse of sex. Sex was "sacred." We entered this sacred precinct sometime after puberty, in that period when we became aware of that mysterious inner self beyond the realm of reason or control. For males at least, masturbation was the first area of life which—even though we may have been told that it was bad—no matter how we tried, we were never able to avoid. We were powerless to keep ourselves pure in spite of our best moral intentions. Sex was the last bastion—the final outpost of mystery, self-transcendence, and sacredness for modern people. Once sex was desacralized, sin ceased to have meaning. Science rendered sin into a harmless biological phenomenon.

Kevin Condon, an Irish Catholic, notes that in ancient

Greece a similar rationalization of the sin occurred, similar to the secularization we are witnessing in our own day. Early Greek writers such as Homer held that wrongdoing has a transcendent dimension because humanity is accountable before the gods. For later Greeks we sin because we are ignorant.

When sin is defined as ignorance, it is a short step to the rationalization of sin. Later, philosophers such as Socrates had an underlying faith in the essential goodness of humanity because ignorance could not be considered as "evil." If humans know good, said Aristotle, they will act rightly. Aristotle speaks of sin as *hamartia*, "missing the mark," somewhere between "misfortune" and "injustice," more akin to "error" or "mistake."

By the time of Christ, the religious understanding of sin had all but disappeared from Greek thought, thus making a fundamental difference between Christianity and paganism. Christianity, following Judaism, saw sin as more than ignorance—sin is transgression, rebellion, and disobedience before God. A sense of sin arises out of our dialogue with God, from the contrast between the fidelity, holiness, and love of God and our impoverished human condition. Sin is a sense of remoteness from God.

One often experiences this distance in times of worship, such as the call-vision of Isaiah in the temple. Face-to-face with God, Isaiah cries, "Woe is me—for I am lost!" Why? "For I am a man of unclean lips, and I dwell in the midst of a people of unclean lips; for my eyes have seen the King, the LORD of hosts!" (Isaiah 6:5). Because Isaiah sees God, he is able to see himself accurately. Then the angel takes a burning coal and cleanses his lips (verses 6-7).

We are reminded of Barth's dictum that "only Christians sin"—only those with a sense of the Almighty have a sense of the seriousness and depth of sin. Only those who encounter God encounter themselves. When Peter perceives the distance between himself and Christ, he cries, "Depart from me, for I am a sinful man, O Lord" (Luke 5:8).

Sin is primarily a religious matter, a matter of the disparity between God and humanity, before it is a moral matter.

> Blessed is he whose transgression is forgiven,
>   whose sin is covered,
> Blessed is the man to whom the LORD imputes no iniquity,
>   and in whose spirit there is no deceit.
>
> When I declared not my sin, my body wasted away
>   through my groaning all day long.
> For day and night thy hand was heavy upon me;
>   my strength was dried up as by the heat of summer.
>
> (Psalm 32:1-4)

For Christians, the prior question of sin is our relationship with God—what this act, this way of life is doing to our relationship with our Creator.

Few passages express this sense of sin as distance from God better than Psalm 51, the Miserere:

> Have mercy on me, O God, according to thy steadfast love;
>   according to thy abundant mercy blot out my transgressions.
> Wash me thoroughly from my iniquity,
>   and cleanse me from my sin!
>
> For I know my transgressions,
>   and my sin is ever before me.
> Against thee, thee only, have I sinned
>   and done that which is evil in thy sight,
> so that thou art justified in thy sentence
>   and blameless in thy judgment.
> Behold, I was brought forth in iniquity,
>   and in sin did my mother conceive me. . . .
>
> Purge me with hyssop, and I shall be clean;
>   wash me, and I shall be whiter than snow. . . .
>
> Cast me not away from thy presence
>   and take not thy holy Spirit from me.
>
> (Psalm 51:1-5, 7, 11)

Traditionally, the church ascribed this psalm to David, to an experience in his life that brought him face-to-face with his own sinfulness. While there may be little historical connection between the psalm and David, the story of David and Bathsheba does connect with what we have been saying about a Christian sense of sin. Let us now turn to that story.

Mid-life Crisis: David and Bathsheba

If ever there had been one in Israel to live a charmed life, it was David. From the beginning he was destined for greatness, born to rule. We met him first in his youth, when he was a shepherd boy. While all Israel shook in its boots before Goliath, this boy knelt down, chose a smooth stone from the brook, placed it in his sling, stared behemoth in the eye and—well, you know the rest of the story.

Israel loved him as she never loved any king before or since. David, slaying giants, parading triumphantly into Jerusalem the unconquerable, brashly renaming it the City of David. David, leading the ark of the Lord in triumphant procession, then stripping and dancing for joy before God and everybody.

David was Israel, her Golden Age when Israel stood astride the whole world and bowed to nobody even as the boy had refused to bow to Goliath. It was Camelot, the Great Society, all as a reflection of one man. David, called by the books of Kings and Samuel, "the righteous one."

In the spring of the year, the time when kings go forth to battle, David sent Joab, and his servants with him, and all Israel; and they ravaged the Ammonites, and besieged Rabbah. But David remained in Jerusalem.

It happened, late one afternoon, when David arose from his couch and was walking upon the roof of the king's house, that he saw from the roof a woman bathing; and the woman was very beautiful. And David sent and inquired about the woman. And one said, "Is not this Bathsheba, the daughter of Eliam, the wife of Uriah the

127

Hittite?" So David sent messengers, and took her; and she came to him, and he lay with her. . . .

In the morning David wrote a letter to Joab, and sent it by the hand of Uriah. In the letter he wrote, "Set Uriah in the forefront of the hardest fighting, and then draw back from him, that he may be struck down, and die." And as Joab was besieging the city, he assigned Uriah to the place where he knew there were valiant men. And the men of the city came out and fought with Joab; and some of the servants of David among the people fell. Uriah the Hittite was slain also. Then Joab sent and told David all the news about the fighting; and he instructed the messenger, "When you have finished telling all the news about the fighting to the king, then, if the king's anger rises, and if he says to you, 'Why did you go so near the city to fight? Did you not know that they would shoot from the wall?' . . . then you shall say, 'Your servant Uriah the Hittite is dead also.' "

So the messenger went, and came and told David all that Joab had sent him to tell. The messenger said to David, "The men gained an advantage over us, and came out against us in the field; but we drove them back to the entrance of the gate. Then the archers shot at your servants from the wall; some of the king's servants are dead; and your servant Uriah the Hittite is dead also." David said to the messenger, "Thus shall you say to Joab, 'Do not let this matter trouble you, for the sword devours now one and now another;' strengthen your attack upon the city, and overthrow it.' And encourage him."

When the wife of Uriah heard that Uriah her husband was dead, she made lamentation for her husband. And when the mourning was over, David sent and brought her to his house, and she became his wife, and bore him a son. But the thing that David had done displeased the LORD.

(II Samuel 11:1-4, 14-27)

"April is the cruelest month," writes T. S. Eliot. Why? Perhaps one must be over forty to know why spring can be cruel. Even for me, before forty, wandering across a university campus on a spring afternoon watching student lovers stroll amidst flowering blossoms—all this love and all this promise and youth and new life can be oddly depressing. It is depressing, if you are no longer young and spring is but a time to experience yourself getting older, to suddenly realize on a spring day that you have more yesterdays on your account than tomorrows. It's the mid-life crisis, isn't it? It's that time when we realize that there are more doors closing behind us than opening in front of us, and we are in the middle—not yet over the hill, but certainly well on the way up the hill. April can be cruel.

It was the spring of the year in Israel; nature was in full bud, and the young kings went out to war. But this year King David stayed home. Each year he had found that it took a bit more effort for him to get in shape for the spring campaign. So he let the younger Joab go without him.

Late that spring afternoon the palace was quiet. The servants had gone, and David was left with himself in the lengthening melancholy of the ending day. Standing there, looking out over deserted streets, alone with his thoughts, quiet—a threatening circumstance for anyone—he gazed across the rooftops of the city he once had the strength to bring to its knees. But that was yesterday.

His eye caught sight of a young woman in her garden, taking her afternoon bath after her chores were done. David knew then that he must have her, take her, conquer her as he had once conquered the city. And he did.

So what did David see that day as he gazed upon lovely Bathsheba that so conquered him? Her body, yes, inflamed him with lust. But more. Did she remind him of other days, days of lost youth, other spring days with the whole world at his feet? Lost youth, lost love, lost opportunity . . .

God knows, any man, any woman too, is ripe for sin at such a time in life on such an afternoon.

The mid-life crisis is as old as David. The poet Dante knew. He begins his *Inferno*, "In the middle of life's journey, I found myself within a dark wood where the straight way is lost."

The toughest, most dangerous part of life's journey,

Dante found, is the middle, when the brightness of early day darkens and night approaches and the straight way can be so easily lost. April is the cruelest month.

Wouldn't it be nice if we could get romantic about this story and treat David and Bathsheba as they might be treated on *Love Boat* or *Fantasy Island*? But that's TV, and this is the Bible. And the Bible is hardly ever romantic. The Bible is realistic.

All self-serving purple prose about dreams, lost youth, love, and longing sours in the face of the facts of David and Bathsheba. The great master David becomes the one who is mastered, made liar. Barth says in *Church Dogmatics* that what impresses him is the sheer shoddiness of it all, this soap opera. "If only he had been caught up in an evil principle and programme! If only he had gone astray and shown his fallibility in a significant entanglement! But as far as he is concerned it is only a trivial intrigue, . . . it is all below his usual level and petty and repulsive."

First, David clumsily attempts to deceive blindly loyal Uriah. But in his refusal to do what is wrong—even when he is drunk—Uriah thwarts David's "brilliant" plan. One lie leads to another until David descends to murder.

I've only heard Balzac or Flaubert tell a story of lust so honestly. How beautifully such a sin begins and how pettily, trivially, mechanically it ends.

Of course, David thought that he was above all that. He was king. The rules are made for other people, commoners such as Uriah, to follow. "The old rules don't count anymore," we tell ourselves. "We are the first generation ever to be confronted with today's moral dilemmas. No one before us felt lust. So we must make up the rules as we go. And who cares, so long as nobody gets hurt?"

G. K. Chesterton once remarked that if a person is walking along and, upon coming to the edge of a cliff, keeps walking, that person will prove the law of gravity rather than break it. Our sad, disordered, broken lives are proving the rules. So it was for David. There are wages to our sin, hell for somebody to pay. The romance ends. An innocent man lies dead on the battlefield; a child is doomed before birth.

And the LORD sent Nathan to David. He came to him, and said to him, "There were two men in a certain city, the one rich and the other poor. The rich man had very many flocks and herds; but the poor man had nothing but one little ewe lamb, which he had bought. And he brought it up, and it grew up with him and with his children; it used to eat of his morsel, and drink from his cup, and lie in his bosom, and it was like a daughter to him. Now there came a traveler to the rich man, and he was unwilling to take one of his own flock or herd to prepare for the wayfarer who had come to him, but he took the poor man's lamb, and prepared it for the man who had come to him." Then David's anger was greatly kindled against the man; and he said to Nathan, "As the LORD lives, the man who has done this deserves to die; and he shall restore the lamb fourfold, because he did this thing, and because he had no pity."

Nathan said to David, "You are the man. Thus says the LORD, the God of Israel, 'I anointed you king over Israel, and I delivered you out of the hand of Saul; and I gave you your master's house, and your master's wives into your bosom, and gave you the house of Israel and of Judah; and if this were too little, I would add to you as much more. Why have you despised the word of the LORD, to do what is evil in his sight? You have smitten Uriah the Hittite with the sword, and have taken his wife to be your wife, and have slain him with the sword of the Ammonites.' . . . Thus says the Lord, 'Behold, I will raise up evil against you out of your own house; and I will take your wives before your eyes, and give them to your neighbor, and he shall lie with your wives in the sight of this sun. For you did it secretly; but I will do this thing before all Israel, and before the sun.' " David said to Nathan, "I have sinned against the LORD." And Nathan said to David, "The LORD also has put away your sin; you shall not die." (II Samuel 12:1-9, 11-13)

The child of David's lust dies; his son Amnon rapes David's daughter; his beloved Absalom murders Amnon and is eventually killed himself. There is hell to pay in the House of David.

Well, of course, David is "only human," we say. Being human is no easy matter, what with our lost dreams and our unfulfilled hopes and our getting older every day. So we are all candidates for the right afternoon in late spring when the sap is rising and we are in a melancholy mood.

We had better pay attention to what God does with those of us who are "only human" like David.

Enter the prophet Nathan. "Let me tell you a little story," says Nathan to King David. (The trouble usually starts with these little stories!) "A rich man had many herds. There was a poor man who had nothing save one beloved lamb. But the arrogant rich man killed the poor man's lamb and served it up to his cronies."

"Criminal!" cried David. "Hang him."

Commie. Humanist. Social deviant. Criminal!

"*You* are the man," said Nathan. David has met the enemy—himself.

David says, "I have sinned."

In an age where we blame it all on society, parents, fate, the educational system—anyone or anything but ourselves—David's confession is refreshing.

"The Lord forgives you," says Nathan.

Perhaps the striking thing about the story is not David's sin (none too dramatic or original), but rather this bold pronouncement of forgiveness, coming so quickly on the heels of so honest a confession. Something in me wouldn't mind seeing the once arrogant David twist on the gibbet for a while. But no, the sin is forgiven—though there are consequences. Our sin is never inconsequential. To say that sin is forgiven is not to say that the past is undone. Even God can't do that.

"Criminal! The Lord forgives you."

The prophetic words thunder over the old man's life,

132

(handwritten margin note: Is he suggesting God willed these things as punishment?)

words spoken so often to Israel: Criminal! The Lord forgives you.

So here is what God does with David and his sin, with you and me and our sin. Shadows darken; a cross is raised over the City of David whereupon hangs the last king of the House of David. What does God do with the motley crew of aging Davids and Bathshebas at the foot of the cross? What about us?

The words thunder forth.

"Criminals!" cry the prophets through the ages.

"Father, forgive them, they don't know what they're doing."

The story of David and Bathsheba does not moralize about sexual ethics or marital fidelity. It rather concerns itself with the prophetic rebuke of a man who has been unfaithful to his relationship with God. David knows: "I have sinned against the Lord" (II Samuel 12:13). "Against thee, thee only, have I sinned" (Psalm 51:4).

Modern theology fails to take sin seriously because it no longer sees sin as "before God." Sin has become a psychological problem, ignorance, immaturity, a failure of adjustment; not adultery, a break in the divine-human relationship. As Kierkegaard says in *The Sickness unto Death*, "The possibility of offense is the dialectical factor that separates Christianity from paganism, and it is rightly included in the Christian definition of sin—in the words 'before God.' "

TEN
THE DENIAL OF EVIL

William James had a theory: We do not run away because we are afraid; we are afraid because we run away. Do we deny evil because we are afraid of its power, or does evil have power because we are afraid to admit its presence? In this chapter we shall explore some of the practical, everyday ways we lie about ourselves. My contention is that (1) we deny evil because we do not have the resources to face it, and (2) the Christian faith is the way to be honest about ourselves and our situation.

Yet we must begin cautiously. Psychoanalysis has long noted that one of the most popular ways of denying the evil in ourselves is to point to it in others. We unconsciously discharge our own guilt by scapegoating; that is, by projecting our sin. Ancient Israel once laid its sins upon the scapegoat and then drove the unfortunate animal into the desert. So we have the Jews, blacks, Poles, Communists, Wasps, capitalists—at some time or another they have all functioned as someone's scapegoat.

So we must be careful. At some point in our conversation about evil, the talk must turn to us. We see clearly only those inadequacies in others which we know to be hidden within ourselves. The moral crusader who goes after the pornographers may be the person who is suppressing those thoughts within himself or herself. The crusader works to destroy all the sinners and, in so doing, unconsciously hopes to destroy the same sin within. Thus Luther advises us first to confess our own sins and then to throw a mantle of charity over the sins of others. A second warning should be raised. As we noted earlier, Karl Marx taught that the ruling class always presents the human condition as bleak and unpromising. Capitalist oppressors spread suspicion of humanity in order to provoke fear of what humanity might do if given freedom. Earlier, Thomas Hobbes gave philosophical justification for governmental oppression and "law and order" at any cost. One could not permit democracy because the masses would go wild if they were unbound. Luther spoke of the rebellious German peasants as "rabble" which must be ruthlessly crushed because they did not respect the divine right of the authorities, conveniently ignoring the rabble within the ruling German princes whose protection he coveted.

When people are overburdened with a vivid sense of sin and evil, they may be slow to throw off their social chains. Why work for a better world if the world is rotten to the core and will probably stay that way in spite of our best efforts? Things will still be in a mess after the revolution, so why try?

In *People of the Lie* Scott Peck notes that "an exclusive focus on the problem of evil is actually extremely dangerous to the soul of the investigator." This is why it is important for us to speak of evil from the standpoint of the Christian story, testing all that we say by its truth. Reformers like Luther understood sin. But they did not always link our inward freedom with our outward freedom, nor did they proclaim the cosmic, social dimensions of Christ's liberating work as much as they preached personal sinfulness.

The story bids us to take seriously the affirmation that Jesus Christ is Lord, that something decisive has happened in the life, death, and resurrection of Jesus. Quietism or Stoic resignation is not an option for the people who live by the whole story.

In my earlier criticism of Americans as people who have generally been oblivious, in theology and social thought, to the reality of evil, I failed to acknowledge that the United States has had some success in creating a relatively free and just society. We are a people who were born of social revolution and who look upon the idea of change as basically good. We therefore have had a greater stake in promoting a view of the essential goodness of people. This view has been productive, so far as it goes, yet it can also be demonic when American delusions of innocence take their toll.

Aspects of the Denial of Evil

The reality of evil is proven by our denial of evil. It seems so strange that those who have lived through the horrors of the present age should deny the reality of the shadow side of life. And yet, the denial is everywhere.

At times we try to *rationalize* evil. Observe our reluctance to use moral and religious language when we talk about evil. We use instead the metaphor of illness. Evil is a kind of sickness, or what appears as sickness, but this is ultimately an unhelpful metaphor. Are we depraved or deprived? As Susan Sontag has pointed out in her book *Illness as Metaphor*, totalitarian movements, whether of the Right or the Left, have been peculiarly inclined to use disease imagery to label nonconformists. Nazis spoke of Jews as a syphilis upon Germany. Every form of social deviation was considered an illness. Today in the United States, criminals are called sick people who are to be not punished but understood, as a doctor understands a patient.

This denial of human participation in evil by calling our sin "sickness" can cut both ways. In the cause of more humane attitudes toward the criminal and the criminal's "treatment" (rather than punishment), the crime is forgotten and the criminal is given over to therapists. We are told that these people have no control over themselves, that they can't help being criminals—society or their parents or something or someone has made them this way. Isn't this demeaning? By denying responsibility we also rob the criminal of his or her humanity. We do not have to take the criminal and his or her actions seriously and are free to manipulate him or her for our purposes.

How does such a view of crime differ from that in the Soviet Union where political dissidents are labeled as insane and treated in mental hospitals? In Anthony Burgess's *A Clockwork Orange*, a young criminal is "treated" by a cadre of social workers and psychologists who, through behavior modification techniques, turn this once violent criminal into a passive automaton who is incapable of sexual assault or other acts of violence. When he is displayed before a group of admiring social engineers, there is loud applause for this product of penal reform. But a red-faced, rotund priest objects, "You have taken away his violence, but have also taken away his humanity." Burgess's point is that even violence is better than no humanity.

Our "treatment" of these "sick" individuals can lead to a most perverse type of social coercion in the name of "treatment."

We anesthetize ourselves to evil through a variety of mechanisms, all of which assure us that evil is not really evil. For instance, we cope with the evil of war by developing theories of "just wars" and "rules" for combat. The military develops detailed procedures for every event in combat. These procedures help to keep soldiers' minds occupied so they have no time to reflect upon the horror in which they are participating. They are not killing; they are simply going by the book, obeying orders, without reflection upon the absurdity of the idea of "rules" for killing.

We indulge in euphemisms in our talk about evil. Dr. Elisabeth Kübler-Ross chides contemporary society and the health care professions for avoiding and denying death, but then, when she speaks of death in her books about death and dying, she speaks of death as "natural," even beautiful. This is another form of rationalization and denial.

People who deny the shadow side of life tend to deny an important part of existence, maybe even the key to our existence. Those who discover that they are frail creatures capable of sin are often better, wiser, more enjoyable people. They have learned to have a sense of humor about themselves, to transcend themselves, and to look at themselves honestly.

Early in my ministry, I became acquainted with a young man who was very active in a conservative religious group on campus. He was a biblical fundamentalist, always having the right Scripture verse or theological answer on the tip of his tongue to cover every situation. He was the epitome of the wholesome young man. But he changed. I noted that he seemed less self-assured, less confident that he always knew the right answer. I told him that I had observed a change in his attitude. Then he confessed that, on a campus religious retreat, he had had sexual intercourse with a young woman. He was shocked that he, a "born-again, biblical Christian could be capable of such sinful behavior." Then I knew what it was that I now liked in him: He had faced the facts about himself. He was now a real person rather than a stilted façade. His religion was now a way of dealing with the facts in his life rather than a means of suppressing and denying the facts.

Jung noted that each of us wears a mask, a "persona," similar to the masks that were worn in ancient Greek drama. This is the face we present to others. It covers our "shadow," our true inner nature which we regard as unacceptable. Generally speaking, Jung felt that the brighter and cleaner the persona, the darker the shadow underneath. The more complex and evasive our mechanisms for denial, the more complex the evil we are seeking to cover.

Frontal assaults upon the reality of evil usually elicit strong defensiveness from us. We expend much psychic energy suppressing our evil, and we do not welcome attempts to uncover our shadow side. Wise pastors find that moralistic preaching or confrontative counseling produces hostility and defensiveness rather than awareness. Because of the subtlety of our denial, a pastor must be thoroughly in touch with his or her own shadow side in order to help people talk about the evil within themselves. If we are not conversant with our own evil and sin, then scapegoating, projection, and self-righteous condemnation are the usual result. The Reformed tradition has tried to honor the biblical dictum that judgment begins with the House of God by beginning Sunday worship with a corporate prayer of confession. The pastor leads the confession because, as one who bears the burden of speaking of sin to others, the pastor is most liable to be the chief of sinners!

Projection is another way of denying the evil in ourselves. This unconscious psychological mechanism occurs whenever part of our personality projects itself onto other people so that we see something in them that is really part of us—our own despised shadow. The more we fear something in ourselves, the more violent and coercive will be our hatred of these "scapegoats" through whom we hope to banish some hated aspect of our subconscious. In every war, the enemy must be portrayed as animalistic, unprincipled, and subhuman so that it will seem less evil for us to be killing such evil people—Commies, Reds, Gooks—not fathers, mothers, sons, and daughters like us.

I once heard a labor union organizer say that he had a tough time organizing southern textile workers because he could not convince these thorough Calvinists that (1) all workers are good and always seek the welfare of their fellow workers, and (2) all management is evil and always oppresses the workers. To their credit, the workers' "Calvinism" would not allow them to project simplistic images onto complex humanity.

The Roots of Denial

In his book *Escape from Evil*, Ernest Becker argued that our natural and inevitable human urge to deny mortality is the root cause of human evil. Our innate fear of both life and death and our vain effort to transcend this fear through various cultural attempts explain why "the imagination of man's heart is evil from his youth" (Genesis 8:21).

Why? Augustine devised the notion of "metaphysical evil," the finitude and limitation of the created universe, to explain the root of human evil.

We humans are, first of all, animals. We may achieve many things in life, but we never escape this primal fact. We exist in a world where life continues only because of a constant bone-crushing, blood-drinking, devouring drama. Human life, for all of its occasional grandeur, builds its home upon the carnage of millions of slain chickens, herds of cattle, sties of pigs, and rivers of fish. As Becker notes, humanity raises its head over a field of corpses, smacks its lips, smiles into the sun, and declares, "Life is good."

Because we are animals, the instinct for survival is strong. Like any other creature, we are driven by the will to consume, survive, and propagate. And yet, unlike the other animals, so far as we know, we humans are cursed with a unique characteristic—we are conscious that we shall die.

From the very beginning, from Adam and Eve, Cain and Abel, and all the rest, we know that we are terminal. We cannot bear the thought. To the Creator, the Psalmist could complain:

> Thou turnest man back to the dust,
>   and sayest, "Turn back, O children of men!"
> For a thousand years in thy sight
>   are but as yesterday when it is past,
>   or as a watch in the night.
>
> Thou dost sweep men away; they are like a dream,
>   like grass which is renewed in the morning:
> in the morning it flourishes and is renewed;
>   in the evening it fades and withers. . . .
>
> For all our days pass away under thy wrath,
>   our years come to an end like a sigh.
> The years of our life are threescore and ten,
>   or even by reason of strength fourscore;
> yet their span is but toil and trouble;
>   they are soon gone, and we fly away. (Psalm 90)

As Barth wrote in *Dogmatics in Outline*, "Some day a company of men will proceed out to a church yard and lower a coffin and everyone will go home; but one will not come back, and that will be me. The seal of death . . . will bury me as a thing that is superfluous and disturbing."

It is not only our mortality that we hate, fear, and attempt to avoid. We fear death, yes, but the thing we fear about death is annihilation, insignificance, "sans teeth, sans eyes, sans taste, sans every thing" (*As You Like It*, Act II, scene 7). We want to know that our lives count, that something of us will endure even in the face of years which come "to an end like a sigh." This is a major promise of any religion, false or true religion—we shall transcend death.

Herein, Becker argues, is the source of human evil. We strive to be something we are not—namely, immortal. Therefore we link our lives to institutions—colleges, churches, clubs, nations—all of which have an aura of immortality about them. We know that we shall die but our church, our school, our fraternity, our nation shall go on. Rather than stand alone, we huddle behind the flag or the president. This is one of the reasons, no doubt, that the state has become so prominent in human history precisely at the time when traditional consolations of religion seem to be in decline. Nationalism becomes a major path to immortality. Hitler promised the "thousand-year Reich." We build bombs and do anything necessary for national defense because the state, our way to immortality, must be preserved at all cost.

This is how Becker can say that humanity's "impossible hopes and desires have heaped evil in the world" (*Escape from Evil*, p. 5). In an effort to achieve the impossible—namely, immortality for mortal beings—we erect a vast array of false gods which we shall defend to the death because they promise to give us eternal life.

So-called "primitive man" attempted to control the life-threatening powers of nature through magic, ritual, and voodoo. It never seemed right that human beings, as marvelous as we are, should be at the mercy of the elements. Magic gave us the possibility of control. Today the conceit continues, not through witch doctors but, in my town at least, through a vast medical establishment which, for millions of dollars a year, promises to deliver that elusive immortality.

What is the largest, most expensive, most overly built edifice in Greenville today? A cathedral? a school? City hall? No. It is Greenville Memorial Hospital, great temple of health and long life in which the high priests go about their rituals with special garments, arcane language, and esoteric wisdom to make us—provided we put enough dollars into the enterprise and ask few questions—immortal. We call the witch doctor's rituals "magic" because we no longer believe that they work; we call our medical technology "science" because we believe that it works.

Certainly our technology works, but only up to a point. At least the witch doctor, when he did no good, usually did no harm either. Our technological failures tend to be more disastrous. We invent the X-ray only to find that it is a major cause of cancer. Some "miracle drugs" produce horrifying birth defects. But the price does not seem too high as long as we believe that it keeps the Fates at bay.

We are shattered when our technology fails to deliver promised bliss. Note how anxious we are to pin an airline crash on "pilot error" or how generous juries are in litigation against doctors—our machines couldn't have failed us; they are immortal. It must be the stupid people who are caring for the machines.

It isn't dying we fear so much as annihilation, powerlessness, oblivion. Technology has assumed such a high place in our lives because the machine gives us power, the closest thing to immortality. The machine offers us control. We can have the name, address, credit record, tax files of anyone with the push of a button. The Nazis were the first to demonstrate how efficiently the machine helps us to control others—even destroy them if we choose.

And yet we are deeply uncomfortable with our technology. Occasionally we lapse into Fabian denigration of the machine, escaping back to nature. But there is no going back. Our horror movies are fixated with technology and its attendant horrors—the "mad scientist" goes too far in his experiments and creates a homicidal monster like Frankenstein or turns himself into the Invisible Man or creates some fly that terrorizes New York. These movie fantasies suggest that the evil is not in our technology. The evil occurs when the scientist abuses a good god, technology.

143

The Military and Money:
Immortality Ideologies

Marx noted how barbaric warfare had become in the modern state. Primitive warfare exacted a comparatively low toll. Battles were conducted by certain limitations of chivalry or military etiquette. But the modern war machine (note that it is a "machine" now) was something else. Marx saw that the modern state solves its internal national problems by siphoning off internal frustration into international military conquests. What better way to keep the disgruntled masses busy than to engage them in a common task of defeating some alien enemy? What better way to forge national solidarity than to take everyone's eyes off domestic affairs and turn them toward the foreigner? (Even as I write this, our government is stepping up its military presence in Lebanon and invading Grenada. The local Marine Corps recruiting office is swamped with eager volunteers.)

As Marx saw it, increased social problems led to an increase in butchery by the state. A huge, professional military bureaucracy was created to perpetuate national fear of alien powers, diverting billions away from internal social problems toward national defense. The military machine promises to generate enough power, enough security to overcome the nation's sense of helplessness. Alas, modern Marxist countries seem just as susceptible to this militaristic temptation as non-Marxist ones, even more so. Observers have long noted the perpetual militaristic stance of Communist countries with civil politicians dressing in military uniforms and great energy expended in nurturing fear among the populace of imminent attack by external enemies. After all our enemies are defeated, the Communists argue, any difficulties here at home will automatically be solved. "Everybody in Cuba is a soldier," proudly declared a Cuban sugar cane worker.

Yet the peculiar barbarity of modern wars has roots deeper than the survival of the modern state. In fact, the creation of the modern state can be explained by reference to the basic human anxiety of death and annihilation. Why else would we so willingly give over basic freedoms to governmental tyranny and bureaucratic control? The state and its military establishment promise to give us what we feel we can have on no other terms—power.

Our wars in behalf of our nation are as vicious as earlier wars over religion because the state is our new religion. We shall defend our state with extraordinary viciousness, even to the point of destroying everything in nuclear holocaust, because we are weak whereas the state is strong. Humanity is the most aggressive, the most gratuitously vicious, of the animals because we are the only animal conscious of death and decay, the only animal engaged in an anxious quest for self-perpetuation. Other animals fight for survival, but we, knowing that no one gets out of this alive and having such grand dreams for ourselves, fight not for survival but for immortality. All wars are *holy* wars.

If the military is our means of achieving power on a national scale, money is our means on a more personal level. Becker calls money "the new universal immortality ideology." How else does one explain the human drive, since primitive times, to accumulate more than we need, to amass useless goods and to display wealth?

Norman O. Brown, in a stunning chapter called "Filthy Lucre" in his book *Life Against Death*, argues that people began to accumulate wealth in imitation of kings. Ancient rulers sought immortality through the erection of buildings, monuments, and columns bearing their image. Only the most precious of stones would do, only the most expensive metals. These stones endured long after the death of the king.

Thus, wealth became not a means for brute survival of

biological life but a mechanism for achieving immortality. Money became magic, sacred. The more one had, the more power and holiness one enjoyed. The first banks were temples. Jesus noted a coin with Caesar's image stamped upon it and took this as a symbol of someone's religious commitment (Matthew 22:21). It was a token for immortality, a false god, a competitor with the real God for human loyalty. You cannot worship this god and the Lord, Jesus said.

Money not only gives us power while we live. It can also be accumulated and passed on so that its power endures even after a person's death, giving a semblance of immortality. Persons may die, but they can endow chairs with their name at universities, erect mausoleums, commission great works of art; in short, use money to deny the determinism of nature.

As older sources of immortality such as family, the church, and magic wane, money becomes the main "immortality ideology." Our mad acquisitiveness, by which we risk health, family, and life itself to accumulate and keep may seem insane until we examine it as a perfectly "rational" way of perpetuating ourselves.

But popular wisdom says, You can't take it with you. This attempt to discredit our greed actually confirms it. We know in our heart of hearts that we can't take it with us; we shall die. This knowledge is not the argument against greed but is its justification. We shall die, yes, but our children shall continue. We can at least pass power on to them in our will. Our name will live on in our sons and daughters who build upon our accumulation and continue the family business after we have gone.

Outsiders wonder why, in the Soviet Union, this allegedly classless society, there is a new prestige class of government bureaucrats who push their children into prestigious schools and plush government careers, accumulate money, and seek special advantages. At the beginning of the Russian Revolution, they may have achieved immortality by merging themselves into the group, the will of the Party, the advance of the state. Now immortality becomes more personal. Get all you can for Number One because you can't take it with you.

Here is the origin of the evil of inequality among persons. Inequality exists, even in allegedly classless societies, because equality diminishes my sense of power, my immortality. Real equality, from this point of view, is not merely economically threatening, but life threatening. If a black man gets the same job I have, it's not that my paycheck may be diminished; it is that *I* am diminished. My one claim to immortality is threatened.

Of course, things were always important to us. But in the modern, one-dimensional world, the importance of things is monumental. Our money is the only way for us to get "saved." We cannot endure economic inequality because we have no other way to perpetuate ourselves. Capitalism, with its two-car garages, video recorders, swimming pools, and all the other conspicuous consumption, is a perfect system for such ritual. Everybody gets a piece of the action; everyone can play at this game of personal accumulation. Unfortunately, capitalism also unleashes a world of constant invidious comparison—I am constantly reminded that you have more than I. Just when I get ahead in my accumulation, I see someone with something better; that is, with more power than I, and so I must begin again. I never have enough. I am never really assured of my immortality through things; therefore, the cycle never ends. This is a cruel and demanding faith.

Socialists sometimes label capitalism as "legalized greed." True, greed is a major manifestation of the capitalist malaise. But it could also be said that socialism is "legalized envy." The socialist is doubly outraged that some have more than others. Economic inequality seems patently unfair because material possessions are the only means of immortality. Through governmental coercion, goods are redistributed. To the socialist, capitalism is grossly wrong because we are not simply talking about money here; we are talking about nothing less than eternal life. Likewise, the capitalist perceives the socialist attack upon "the free-enterprise system" as an attack upon "our American way of life." Actually, it is an attack upon our American way of eternal life. Socialists and capitalists who recognize no transcendent, immaterial values have no other way to transcend the human condition except through money, so their economic arguments are especially bloody.

Because modern people recognize only visible, tangible, material immortality, we see why many modern Christian theologians have become, of late, preoccupied wth economic rather than theological concerns. Most liberation theologians rely on a Marxist interpretation of history and human nature, which means an essentially materialistic interpretation of everything. Political and economic issues become crucially important for people who recognize no other way of being human and perpetuating humanity than by acquiring things.

Christianity is a threat to both capitalism and communism—at least when it takes its own message seriously. One reason that primitive Christians could part with material possessions—even life itself—so cheerfully was that they had their eyes fixed upon "the city which has foundations, whose builder and maker is God" (Hebrews 11:10). As Ernest Becker notes, "Primitive Christianity is one of the few ideologies that has kept alive the idea of the invisible dimension of nature and the priority of this dimension for assuring immortality" (*Escape from Evil*, p. 86). The only salvation worth having is salvation from our fear of death and our terror of insignificance. Christianity historically has offered this possibility. It holds that it is futile to try to extricate humanity from evil and injustice while fear of death remains in the heart. "He who finds his life will lose it. And he who loses his life for my sake will find it," says

Christ (Matthew 10:39 and parallels). We cannot stop exploitation, denial, or inequality as long as life is interested only in preserving life.

Christianity is subversive to any one-dimensional world view which sees the world and people in only materialistic terms, any ideology which reduces human beings to simple matters of race, class, producers, or consumers. We avoid the Christian claim that calls us to renounce possessions, class, race, gender, and any other materialistic, totemistic claim upon our lives because we have simply denied the existence of any realm other than the material. Now we are free to pursue wealth and its powers with a vengeance and wholehearted dedication that was unknown to our forebears.

Because of our denial, we dare not admit to the limitations of the economic and the political; we dare not admit to hungers which are deeper than the material; we dare not admit to the impotence of our things to save us. Theologians of the Right assure us that it is utterly essential that capitalism be preserved for the good of Christianity. Theologians of the Left say that there is no greater cause for the Christian than to work for "economic justice" and "fair distribution of wealth." After all, what else is worth working for? We develop theologies based upon a claim for the uniqueness of a sexual or racial perspective because sex and race become very important for people who define themselves in exclusively material, visible categories. Anyone who suggests another dimension of life is dismissed as a hopeless reactionary, woefully out of touch with modern life. What he or she is out of touch with is not so much modern life as modern gods. Once we are without God, we make do with what is left, because we are frightened, naked, and alone.

I believe that Becker helps us to focus upon the root of our sin in a way which is true to the way the Bible depicts us. Sometimes we have thought of sin as the violation of codes, laws, and commands. But these are the symptoms rather than the cause. For Augustine, sin was perverted will, disordered love, goodness distorted. But even this view fails to account for the independent, vicious forcefulness of our sin. Sometimes sin has been seen as wrong choices; but this is too rationalistic, too moralistic and episodic. All of these views see sin as a misuse of human freedom.

But Becker says sin is our inappropriate response to our awareness of our human bondage to death and decay. Our evil arises out of our search for good. As Reinhold Niebuhr says, the majority of modern interpretations of human life and history are "a clever contrivance of human pride to obscure the weakness and the insecurity of man" (*Faith and History: A Comparison of Christian and Modern Views of History*).

A Case in Point: Marxism

The fundamental problem of Marxism as a social philosophy is its view of human nature. The Marxists teach that human beings are slaves because of the unjust power of others. Supposedly, in some state of primitive communism, such power was absent and people were contented and free. But, as we have argued, the real sources of human injustice and bondage are with humanity from the very first, and there is no "fall" as some historical event.

For the Marxists, conservative social theory stresses the rottenness of human nature in order to excuse coercion by the state and economic interests. Sin and evil are structural, social, systemic problems. But there is a mass of psychological evidence to suggest that human beings are in bondage even before they get to society. We carry within ourselves the bondage that leads to our willingness to be subjected to the state or the economy or whatever else promises to save us. Our envy, destructiveness, and violent tendencies have to do first with who we are as human beings and only secondarily and derivatively with the sorts of societies which we create.

Human history is a saga of our attempts to work out our human inadequacies on someone else—relatively harmlessly in our daily contacts with others, viciously and destructively when we are in groups who have power. The Marxists, following the Rousseauist "noble savage" myth, see human nature as a blank slate, neutral, even good down deep. If there is evil in the world, the Marxist says it is the result of social institutions that corrupt our primal purity. Capitalism, it is said, simply takes these pure individuals and, through its institutions, encourages hate, envy, competition, degradation, and all other kinds of human misery. Change the institutions, change the system, and innate human goodness shall flower.

Marxism has always appealed to intellectuals. It begins with a delightfully simple view of human nature and then wonders how the wicked world corrupted this inborn innocence. Marxism is never too interested in psychology because it sees the human psyche as a rather uninteresting, flattened terrain. Human beings have only a few basic needs, mostly economic in nature. Sociology is the real fixation of Marxism because the source of corruption is somewhere in society, economic systems, or politics.

Amazingly, Marxists seem never troubled by the lack of empirical evidence for their philosophy. The commonplace observation that Marxist regimes repress rather than liberate their citizens, that their revolutions do not abolish class and privilege, seem not to deter Marxists from holding an absurdly optimistic view of human nature. Marxism, purporting to be based on scientific observation, seems utterly oblivious to empirical realities.

"Well, we are not talking about the kind of Marxism

that exists in the Soviet Union," they say. "We are talking about a Marxism that exists perhaps in some South American countries, maybe not even there."

The fact is, their Communist paradise exists in their imaginations. Our unfreedom is within us before it has a chance to be outside us. Their philosophy is a factory of slogans and banners that have proved well-suited to the cynical purposes of a host of petty tyrants, dictators, and repressive governments. Because society is said to be evil, anyone who proposes to change that society for the better is free from moral restraints to coerce that society into change. Never mind that the Marxist dream has never been achieved, even after the death of millions in concentration camps, purges, "re-education" campaigns, and revolutions.

But is it so amazing that the myth of the recovery of primal innocence, first stated by Rousseau, restated by Marx, continues to gather the allegiance of millions? One can understand many people being attracted to it on the basis of its simplicity—here is a straightforward solution to some complicated, ancient problems. One can understand how intellectuals, theologians, and university professors could be enamored of the Communist myth—they have so little influence in society and are bound to be attracted to anything that promises to give them power to change others, particularly if it comes in the form of some grand and untested dream for human betterment. And yes, one can understand how the dictators and tyrants are attracted to the Communist dream, for every dictator from Augustus to Hitler to Mao has known the power of the grand idea, the noble dream, the unrealized theory as a means of achieving totalitarian control of other human beings—"peace with justice." But what is one to make of the millions who march behind this repressive banner?

The answer lies in human nature itself. As we have said, we are frightened creatures who know that we are mortal. We will therefore give ourselves to any idea, any leader, any symbol that promises to deliver us from our feelings of powerlessness and our fear of annihilation. We desperately need to believe that we are basically good people who have been corrupted by an unjust society. We want to believe that, given the proper social tinkering, given a new regime in city hall, we shall cure what ails us. We will give ourselves to any slogan or march to our death behind any banner which enhances our self-esteem. We are willing to let our freedom, our rights, our individuality die in order not to die. "Power to the people." That's all we want—power, power to change our weakness and fear into confidence. With gun in hand and banners unfurled, we shall have this dream of immortality even if we must jail thousands of "enemies of the state" or blow ourselves to bits to have it.

The peculiar tragedy of Marxism is its stubborn refusal to look at the facts. It presumes to see so much in history while failing to see the most self-evident of historical facts—human nature is complex, difficult, and fallen. Even after the best of revolutions, one is still stuck with human nature, a nature which is often terribly frightened and therefore terribly violent, deceptive, and destructive. Anyone who wants to change the world for the better must begin by being honest about human nature.

And yet, conservatives, in their criticism of the Marxists, are not facing the facts either. Humanity may be caught in a tangled web of sin, rebellion, inhumanity, and self-destructiveness. But, in a sense, this sin and evil arise out of humanity's never-ceasing energy to make something of itself, to rise above its plight, to perpetuate the good which we experience only fleetingly in ourselves and make it a more permanent part of our world. Our desire to be somebody is what Becker calls the "vital lie"—the notion that our frail lives can be extended through our own actions. Out of this vitality we have created both the Sistine Chapel and Buchenwald. Which shall it be for us?

Conservatives must admit that the hate, destruction, inhumanity, envy, and self-deception that we see in humanity are not basic parts of human nature but are rather the symptoms that arise out of our fear of death and impotence. If we could somehow come to terms with our mortality rather than deny it, if we could somehow transcend our anxiety over our condition as animals, then the evils we inflict upon ourselves and others could be dealt with. It is out of fear that we have built both nuclear weapons and the United Nations. Which shall it be for us?

By tracing our miseries to our conflicts within ourselves, we at least have begun to be honest about our situation. It is only by way of this honesty that we can begin to change the world for the better. If we could better understand why we sell our freedom for the security of the state, why we are so susceptible to the appeal of the tyrant and demigogue, or, on the other hand, why we must continue to keep down and oppress the legitimate aspirations of the poor and the powerless, then we might be on the path to freedom. We could turn our energies away from complex and potentially destructive forms of denial toward a furtherance of life as it is and as God means it to be.

Keeping Hope and Honesty in Tension

The dilemma in which we find ourselves is how to admit to the reality of evil in human life, how to be honest about the empirical data on humanity which show that we are now and always have been horribly destructive creatures, and yet not lapse into utter cynicism and despair.

In the seventeenth century, as modern nations were taking form, European philosophers attempted to justify the absolutism of the new monarchies by an appeal to human nature. Thomas Hobbes (1588–1679) cited the violence and disorder of the English Civil War as evidence that human nature in its natural state was "solitary, poor, nasty, brutish and short." In order to hold their natural tendencies in check, people come to a kind of "contract" whereby they surrender some of their freedom into the hands of a ruler. This ruler must have absolute power; otherwise, chaos would result.

Though Hobbes had little direct influence on later political thought, he was one of the first in a long line of modern political theorists who sought to protect society from the evil actions of individuals by giving power to the state. Modern history has shown that the problem of political evil is not solved by simply eliminating democratic chaos in favor of totalitarian order. Evil transfers from the mob to the bureaucracy—anonymous, faceless tyranny which justifies its brutality and injustice by appeals to slogans which conceal its cynical oppression of the human spirit.

Such bureaucratic oppression is frequently justified on the basis of the inherent evil in human nature: We need a strong central government in order to keep the citizens from running wild in the streets. If human nature is as bad as it seems, then we must coerce people into what we define as the "good life"—the worker's paradise, the classless society, the free enterprise system—or else lapse into despair over the possibility of a more humane world.

Is it possible to be sober about our real situation as human beings and yet still affirm that there is nothing within us that prevents us from taking some control of our destiny and making the world a more sane place for our young? Is it possible to rise above the simple-minded optimism which is killing humanism today—to be accurately pessimistic and humanistic at the same time? Pessimism is a form of agnosticism which looks upon the facts of human nature and sees no certain prospect for human future. On the other hand, cynicism is a peculiar form of human sloth and arrogance which takes a superficial look at human nature and, on the face of it, refuses to entertain the possibility of hope because of the courage required to hope when humanity is as it is. Can cynicism be avoided?

Hobbes quoted frequently from the Bible in his writing, but he was never influenced by it. He was a practical modern atheist. Hobbes understood the wretchedness of humanity. But without a God, what could one do with the human situation except (1) deny that humanity was as bad as the evidence suggested, or (2) urge authoritarian government which would keep human nature in check?

There is another alternative.

ELEVEN
THE PROBLEM OF SUFFERING

When most of us think about evil, we think about suffering. Suffering is the companion of evil, the human result of a confrontation with evil in any of its guises. Why do people suffer? Why are there sickness, heartache, the pain of Tom Brown and the agony of Willie Earle, the anguish and the despair?

I have left this question until the end, thinking that suffering can be explored only after asking the question of sin and evil, only after telling the story of the One who confronts and defeats evil. The difficulty in this chapter is not only to talk about suffering in a compassionate and realistic way but in a Christian way—a way which is faithful to the story of what suffering does to Jesus and what Jesus does with suffering.

We begin with an episode on the way to the cross, an illuminating conversation between Jesus and his disciples concerning the place of suffering within the cost of discipleship.

Now when Jesus came into the district of Caesarea Philippi, he asked his disciples, "Who do men say that the Son of man is?" And they said, "Some say John the Baptist, others say Elijah, and others Jeremiah or one of the prophets." He said to them, "But who do you say that I am?" Simon Peter replied, "You are the Christ, the Son of the living God." . . .

From that time Jesus began to show his disciples that he must go to Jerusalem and suffer many things from the elders and chief priests and scribes, and be killed and on the third day be raised. And Peter took him and began to rebuke him, saying, "God forbid, Lord! This shall never happen to you." But he turned and said to Peter, "Get behind me, Satan! You are a hindrance to me; for you are not on the side of God, but of men."

 Ego

Then Jesus told his disciples, "If any man would come after me, let him deny himself and take up his cross and follow me. For whoever would save his life will lose it, and whoever loses his life for my sake will find it. For what will it profit a man, if he gains the whole world and forfeits his life? Or what shall a man give in return for his life?"

(Matthew 16:13-16, 21-26)

It is difficult to know who Jesus is. He was rejected, in part, because he failed to meet conventional messianic expectations. Who is he? When asked, Peter responds, "You are the Christ, the Son of the living God." You are the long-awaited Messiah who shall deliver us from suffering, the One who shall raise an army and expel our Roman oppressors, the One who shall heal and put all things right, the One who shall finally set us up in our place.

As so often happens with Jesus, the conversation takes an unexpected turn. "From that time Jesus began to show his disciples that he must go to Jerusalem and suffer many things . . . and be killed." The response of Peter, the church, is typical and perennial: "God forbid, Lord! This shall never happen to you."

Jesus says that Peter's attempt to protect him is satanic. We, the disciples, the church, follow Jesus not only as his disciples but as those devilish ones who seek cushions rather than crosses—those who are forever shocked that the Savior is also the sufferer. As Mark tells the story, Jesus is on the way to Jerusalem—not on the way to triumph and glory—but on the way to the cross

158

and death. "Jesus was walking ahead of them," Mark says, "and they were amazed, and those who followed were afraid" (Mark 10:32).

That's where Jesus always is with us in relation to suffering, "ahead of us." In spite of our best efforts to follow, we are always amazed, even afraid. It never seems right that one so good as Jesus, one so close to God (or for that matter, one so good as we disciples) should be walking toward the capital city where "they will mock him, and spit upon him, and scourge him, and kill him" (Mark 10:34).

Again and again Jesus must teach us that "the Son of man must suffer many things, and be rejected . . . and be killed" (Mark 8:31). If we follow this Messiah, if we walk with him, we must walk behind him as he goes ahead of us into suffering. If we discuss the mystery of suffering and pain in a Christian way, we must discuss it on the way to the Place of the Skull, where the one who saves will "suffer many things, and be rejected . . . and be killed."

The Nature of Suffering

Today's most popular preachers—the Pat Robertsons, Oral Robertses, and Robert Schullers of TV land—preach sermons that are preoccupied with suffering. In varying styles and theologies, they offer deliverance—physical, economic, psychological, and spiritual. While there is more than a touch of manipulation in their message, and while we may fault them for victimizing people with their constant appeals for money, these preachers stick to the basic questions. The rest of us who preach the Gospel on a regular basis might learn from them—if Christianity has no response to the suffering of the world, it isn't relevant. Or, as Monika Hellwig has said, if it doesn't play in a cancer ward or a shoddy nursing home for the elderly, whatever it is, it isn't good news.

But in what way is the Gospel the Good News of Jesus

159

and not simply the good news of delusion and false consolation?

What does it mean to suffer? When we speak of suffering we often mean that we are in pain. But in itself pain cannot be regarded as unmitigated evil. Pain is part of life, human life or any other. The dead cannot feel pain. Without pain, human beings would probably self-destruct. A parent protects a child from a serious burn by holding the child's hand near a hot stove and saying, "Hurt!" The child, feeling the sensation of heat, makes the connection and avoids contact with the stove.

"Where does it hurt?" the doctor asks. Pain is a valuable diagnostic tool. A person who feels no physical pain is in a sad and dangerous condition. Also, pain helps to immobilize the body during periods of serious illness so the body's curative processes can work to restore health.

On a more dynamic level, pain can also function to awaken compassion. We feel the suffering of others as if it were our own. Empathy is somewhat selfish since the pain we are feeling is the result of putting ourselves in the place of another. We hurt more at the thought of our pain than at the thought of the other person's affliction. But such empathy sometimes mobilizes us to find cures for dreaded illness and ways to avoid similar pain.

God has created a world in which pain is part of life. We come into the world through the pain of our mothers and we depart through suffering of our own. Like the young Buddha, we may be shielded from pain for many years, but at some point we must admit that the Buddha was right: "Life is suffering."

Today there is great resentment toward pain in our culture. We have so many new methods of alleviating pain. Our medical establishment has, even if unintentionally, led us to believe that all pain can be eradicated and, by implication, that any pain is unjustified and without positive significance. We have made pain utterly

160

meaningless. But pain, in itself, is not necessarily an unmitigated evil.

Without pain, how could humanity have developed and progressed? A developmental theodicy like that of Irenaeus, John Hick, or Norman Pittenger (chapter 4) questions what kind of humanity would result from a world without hunger, thirst, excessive heat and cold. Activities such as hunting, farming, and house building, by which we fend off painful conditions, would be pointless. There would be no need for exertion, ingenuity, and creativity because there would be no problems to be solved or difficulties to be overcome. There would be nothing to avoid and nothing to seek, no need for cooperation or stimulus for the development of culture and civilization. A hedonistic paradise would leave little room for the development of all those qualities we regard as essential to human life. The Irenaean conception that the world is a place of soul making suggests that we are here not merely to avoid pain and to seek pleasure but also to develop and to move closer to God. Suffering is a part of the price we pay for our humanity and our freedom.

We need only imagine the implications of a world without pain and suffering to respond to the question of why God does not remove pain from human life. What sort of world would remain? Could we conceive of human life without nervous systems, without physicality? The elimination of all conflict and attendant pain would be achieved at a high price.

We feel pain because God has not created us to be machines. It is not that God has created an imperfect machine which, for all its glory, still feels pain. It is that God has created an animal whose life is more than mere production and consumption. An alternative world with a markedly alternative humanity would not be the world or the humanity which we know, would not be the people whom God has chosen for communion. Our modern assumption of the meaninglessness and the pointlessness

161

of pain must be reexamined with a view toward the ultimate purpose of human existence.

Imagine an anesthetic world without pain. No immoral act would have bad consequences. If I socked my neighbor in the nose, no one would be hurt, though I would still be an aggressor. In such a world, there would be no moral value, for to act wrongly means to hurt someone or God. Love, which we usually define as fidelity in the midst of struggle and sacrifice, would have no meaning. If God wants people of depth and character, what sort of hedonistic, pain-free world could God have created?

Yet there is a danger in being too positive about pain. Earlier we warned against the tendency to argue that evil is really good. When confronted with sickness and attendant pain, Jesus did not simply philosophize about the pain as evidence of the way the world was wisely constructed; rather, he charged that the illness was the work of Satan (Luke 13:16), something to be rebuked and driven out. Paul fervently prayed that his "thorn in the flesh" be removed (II Corinthians 12:7-9), knowing that he could do more for God if he were healthy than if he were sick.

This view flies in the face of much conventional wisdom about pain. "God never puts more on us than we can bear" is a cliché that assumes that God is the author of suffering, not its enemy. We all know people whom great pain has crushed rather than strengthened. The homiletical analogy that steel must be tempered by fire in order to make it strong is inappropriate—we are not made of iron. Suffering produces despair and cynicism as often as it produces strength and determination. If suffering is God's way of teaching, it is a poor method of instruction. So much suffering seems utterly without meaning. What is a nine-year-old child dying of leukemia to learn from her pain?

Certainly some pain helps us to adapt. But too much

162

pain is by no means proportional to the gravity of the danger—a toothache, for instance. Some pain in no way contributes to the betterment of a person's life. The only lesson to be learned is that life is terribly confusing and unfair. Pain fulfilled little adaptive function in all the centuries before medical science developed to such a level as to be able to use it as a diagnostic tool. While some pain is helpful and even essential, need the world contain so much of it and in such apparently pointless and unedifying situations?

Besides, what about the pain of animals? If pain were an exclusively human phenomenon, we might agree that it does contribute to the process of soul making. But animals feel pain as much as humans. How can such agony be called good?   *Maybe animals have souls, too*

Thus we are stuck with a cruel paradox: Pain is part of animal life, human or otherwise, part of the necessary apparatus of adaptation; yet pain, particularly chronic, excessive pain, is evil and should be resisted. Like sex, money, power, knowledge—all gifts of God's good creation—pain can also be the demonic occasion for much evil.

One person's pain from cancer causes her to feel self-pity, resentment toward others, and cynicism. Another person's cancer mobilizes her to form the first cancer support group in her community, to seek out other victims and encourage them not to lose hope.

What is the difference? Both humans and animals feel pain, but only humans find meaning—positive or negative meaning—in pain. A kidney stone is as painful as a difficult childbirth, but we experience the pain in quite different ways. One is meaningful; the other is not. A physician who had served in World War II observed that the same injury suffered in training camp and then on the battlefield appeared to produce less pain on the battlefield. In the heat of battle, with everyone working toward the same goal, the pain of the injury was mitigated by other factors.

Suffering is a natural, physical sensation. But sometimes suffering has a mental, psychological, and spiritual counterpart—anguish. In themselves, our finitude, weakness, and physicality are not evil. They are part of the way we are. To wish otherwise is to wish to be who we are not. The problem is not simply pain—that we feel pain or that some pain is too much—but that we find so little meaning in some pain.

Anguish is the concomitant of meaningless pain. It divides the pain of childbirth from the pain of cancer. It often inflicts people who are not in physical pain. In affluent, prosperous countries, why are so many people driven to drug addiction, marital stress, and suicide? As a pastor, I find the anguish caused in a family because of an alcoholic to be a greater challenge to my faith and theirs than the anguish caused when someone in a family has terminal cancer. Some of the most intense, complex suffering appears to be nonphysical, the result of anguish caused by meaninglessness.

 Suffering has little inherent value except as something which God is working to overcome—something which, even as bad as it is, God is able to use for his purposes. Even as God is not defeated by our sin, God is not defeated by the presence of suffering—not because pain is good but because God is good.

The problem, it seems to me, is not that suffering and pain exist in the world and that we feel them. The real problem is that suffering seems so random and so meaningless, crushing people as often as it ennobles them, falling upon the undeserving and deserving alike.

We must reject any response which rationalizes someone's misery by saying, "You suffer because you have been bad and deserve to suffer" or "This suffering is God's will." That would be to call evil good.

Suffering and pain, particularly in their undeserved,

excessive, and chronic forms, are an awesome mystery. Suffering falls with a kind of haphazardness and inequality upon people. It is often incredibly unfair, a great mystery among other mysteries which remind us that there is always a "beyond" in even our best and most reasoned explications of the world.

Pain is so threatening to us, in part, because it is the ultimate challenge to our self-idolatry: the accusing, relentless forewarning of our ever-impending death. It produces anxiety because it is a concrete, unavoidable reminder that we are frail, physical creatures who shall die. Like any reminder of our finitude, pain presents us with the opportunity either to turn aside into fantasy, false hope, or despair, or else turn toward God.

Pain is paradoxical. While we may not be able to say that our suffering is "God's will," many can attest that their suffering has caused them to focus their lives; has brought them closer to God; has strengthened their character in a way in which, looking back, they could claim that God's will was done even in the midst of their suffering. One cannot read the biography of some great person, viewing how strength and wisdom are often born in adversity, without agreeing with Paul that "suffering produces endurance, and endurance produces character, and character produces hope" (Romans 5:3-4).

But pain can lead to a loss of meaning rather than to an increase in meaning. It can be the force that drives us toward hell rather than into the arms of God.

Pain is the satanic invitation to believe that we are nobody, that our lives mean nothing, that our years, in spite of their intermittent joys, are full of pain, and then "come to an end like a sigh" (Psalm 90:9). Pain is also the satanic invitation to see ourselves as derelict, forsaken creatures who have been abandoned by God.

My God, my God, why has thou forsaken me? Why art thou so far from helping me, from the words of my groaning?

165

O my God, I cry by day, but thou dost not answer;
and by night, but find no rest. (Psalm 22:1-2)

Read rest of Psalm 22 - good ending.

How could a loving God desert his world in its moments of pain? Where is God in all this suffering?

Jesus and Pain

In *Man's Search for Meaning*, Viktor Frankl noted that "suffering ceases to be suffering in some way the moment it finds meaning."

Christians claim that suffering has meaning only as we enter into our pain as Christ entered into his. The story of Christ gives significance to our stories of suffering. Watching him hanging on the cross, blessing thieves, forgiving his tormentors, we note he suffered without regard for himself in contrast to the way our suffering often drives us ever deeper into ourselves.

When the doctor tells us that we are suffering from heart disease, we ask, *Why did this happen to me?* without a thought for all the sufferers who have preceded and shall follow us in illness. And this is natural.

Natural too is the way we live our lives so as to maximize our pleasure and minimize our pain. We avoid commitments to others for fear that they will betray our trust and cause us anguish. We keep silent and play along with the crowd rather than risk public disapproval. We stand by and watch injustice lest we become its next victim. Most of us are practical hedonists, and this is natural.

Utterly unnatural is the response of Jesus to suffering. His is a story of one who first engages the suffering of others not with philosophical argument or pious platitudes, but with active rebuke and firm compassion. Then he engages his own suffering with human anguish mixed with divine determination. He enjoyed pain no more than we. He wept, he recoiled, he asked to be delivered from

166

suffering three times. Feeling alienated, he cried, "My God, my God, why have you forsaken me?"

Lepers, the sick, the poor, and the oppressed crowded around him. He touched them, healed them, promised them a place at the center of his coming kingdom. Ultimately, he did more than touch them in their pain; *he became one of them*, the Messiah who saves through suffering.

He knew all about the pain of the world, even before he came to his cross. His life practically began in exile as he and his family were refugees in Egypt during the slaughter of the innocents. His baptism foreshadowed his death (Luke 12:50). For him, the cup of thanksgiving was also the cup of blood. The shadow of the cross falls over every episode of his life. His people rejected him; religious leaders condemned him; disciples forsook him and fled. Then, on the cross, he entered the dark, lonely sanctuary of pain before death. In the face of this evil, Jesus offered no philosophical response, no theodicy. Rather, his response was both concrete and practical—he spoke to God as Father, a Father who knows when even a sparrow falls to the ground, who feels pain and has pity. Early in our history, the church fought to maintain the idea that God suffers (Patripassianism). We do this God no favor by depicting him as aloof, detached, and distant. It makes a difference to this God. This God hurts.

Christianity has no interesting answer for suffering. All it has is a practical, concrete way of dealing with suffering. This faith neither denies the pain, explains it away, nor accepts it with Stoic indifference. What is interesting about Christianity is how it handles suffering, how it uses it.

The cross is the sign of what God does with suffering. God answers the problem of human pain by identification, by participation, by *being there*.

If Jesus had simply lived a good, full, happy life and had died peacefully in his sleep one night or had ascended to

167

heaven on a golden chariot, bypassing the cross and death, there would be nothing particularly helpful in our claim that Jesus is the Messiah. An ancient hymn proclaims, "God reigns from a tree." His crown is one of thorns; his throne, a cross. He gains his kingdom through pain, embracing humanity even in the midst of his own dereliction. "Where was God when my son was killed?" a woman asked. Her pastor answered, "Just where he was when his own Son was killed."

You have probably read the passage from Elie Wiesel's *Night*, in which a child was hanged by the Nazis. Because of the child's weight, it took him longer to die: "For more than half an hour he stayed there, struggling between life and death. . . . His tongue still red, his eyes not yet dazed. Behind I heard [a] man asking: 'Where is God now?' I heard a voice within me answer him: Where is He? Here He is—He is hanging here on this gallows."

To see Jesus on the cross is to receive encouragement. We look "to Jesus the pioneer and perfecter of our faith" (Hebrews 12:2), a pioneer who has preceded us in pain, who was perfected in suffering. We fearfully follow as his first disciples, as he goes ahead of us, ahead to where he "must suffer . . . and be rejected . . . and be killed" (Mark 8:31). We follow him down no pathway of pain which he has not walked before us.

To say that "in Christ God was reconciling the world to himself" (II Corinthians 5:19) is to say that God has willingly invaded our history, taking upon himself our dilemma. In the words of the spiritual, "Nobody knows the trouble I see, Nobody knows the trouble I see, Nobody knows but Jesus, Glory Hallelujah."

But the Christian claim is not simply that God in Christ bears suffering, but that in Christ, suffering is overcome. Suffering is not redemptive, but it raises the question to which redemption in Christ is the answer. Because the cross, horrible sign of evil and suffering, has been transformed into a sign of victory, early Christians could speak of their pain as cleansing, illumination, and vocation—not because of the pain itself, but rather because of what God does with the pain.

The nonbeliever wants to know, Why did this happen to me? What did I do to deserve such anguish? Of course the answer is usually nothing. You did nothing to deserve your pain, so your suffering is without cause, justification, or meaning.

The Christian's question in the face of pain will be different. It will arise out of his or her curiosity: *What is God doing with my pain?* We do not really know why the blow was struck any more than we know why sin, evil, injustice, and tragedy exist in such a good and beautiful world. We need not suppress our feelings of anger, injustice, self-pity, or dereliction. Jesus could not hide his anguish; neither can we. But one thing we can do is inquire what God may be doing in our pain. Why is God here with us, hanging here on this cross which should rightly be ours alone?

Because the world seeks only happiness, believing the lie that we can have life without having pain, the world is always shocked by the arrival of pain as if it were something horribly unfair, unexpected, and improbable. But the Christian was never encouraged to seek happiness in itself. We were never promised a rose garden. We were only promised that, in the end, we should have communion with the One who created us, loved us, suffered with and for us, so that he might always have and enjoy us. In the end, our hope is not just that we should be happy, but that we should be good—that we should be persons of character and depth who bear the divine image well.

So, in our pain, we ask the same questions which the Story has taught us to ask throughout our lives—in the midst of good times and bad, opportunities and tragedies. What is God doing now? What is God doing here? If we can get some glimmer of that, it is light enough for the dark journey through suffering. We can manage, somehow, if someone is there to walk with us.

"Although the fig tree shall not blossom," cries the prophet, "yet I will rejoice in the LORD, I will joy in the God of my salvation" (Habakkuk 3:17, 18 KJV). Or, as suffering Job declared, "Though he slay me, yet will I trust in him" (Job 13:15 KJV).

We look at the cross of Jesus and see what God is up to in the world. We look at our own crosses and see what we, as his disciples, are to be up to in the world, we who have been invited to take up our cross daily and follow a path which nobody wants to go.

Some religions measure themselves by the degree of bliss they evoke in adherents, the number of souls they attract, the magnitude of their holy buildings. Christianity measures itself by the weight of crosses it bears in the name of its crucified God. "For where man's strength ends, God's strength begins. . . . For where man's strength begins, God's strength ends" was the way Luther expressed the paradox of a faith which gains its victories through suffering. "The cross puts everything to the test," he said.

The disciples learned that day on the road to Caesarea Philippi that we do not follow this Lord except toward places where he (and we) "must suffer many things, and be rejected . . . and be killed" (Mark 8:31). The cross we are to bear is the one we willingly take up on our shoulders—the scorn we willingly bear for the sake of truth; the cancer we endure, not in defeat and denial, but as an opportunity for witness; the hurt we accept as an expected response wherever evil is challenged, as disciplines of discipleship.

A few years ago, Gerald Forshé told of how he and his family chose to stay in a racially changing Chicago neighborhood even after all the other white residents fled to the suburbs. The neighborhood declined. Members of the family suffered abuse and harassment from some of their neighbors and were forsaken by their white friends. Still, they stayed, as a Christian witness.

One day they returned to their home to find it had been burglarized and vandalized. They walked from room to room, their eyes filling with tears as they saw their possessions and family keepsakes had been stolen or destroyed.

Surveying the heartbreaking scene, Forshé heard a popular tune of the 1950s rising in his brain. A paraphrase of the words became clear:

It is no secret what God can do,
What he did to Jesus, he'll do to you.

Of course the world, not God, does this. But the words are right—those who dare to take up Jesus also take up the cross. In the world, we live to die. We come to Jesus, dying to live. "For the sake of Christ, then, I am content with weakness, insults, hardships, persecution, and calamities; for when I am weak, then I am strong" (II Corinthians 12:10).

This is the "theology of the cross" which Luther, following Paul, saw at the heart of our faith. It is a great help to see our sufferings as participation in the suffering of Christ, as marks of discipleship, and as witness to our solidarity with Christ in his solidarity with humanity.

The theology of the cross is calloused and perverted when it is applied to the suffering of others, when we say, in effect, "Suffer, suffer, this is what Christ wants for you. Rejoice, your suffering puts you close to Jesus." The theology of the cross can lead to complacency and resignation when not wedded with compassion. Jesus is not only the Crucified One, he is also the despised Samaritan who not only pities those who bleed in the ditch, but actively binds their wounds, risks all, and continues to care for them.

Our own suffering is an occasion to turn close to God and seek the One who turns close to us in our suffering.

The suffering of others is an occasion for us to stand beside them and to proclaim the presence of a God, who even in the midst of this evil, is with us. Another's pain is also an occasion for us to be like Jesus and rebuke evil, work for its defeat, eradicate the cause of the pain.

Compassion

Christ calls us to "love one another as I have loved you." This is a big order when we have been loved by One who was willing to go to a cross to love us.

We face the reality of evil because we are called to be compassionate. But we can't be compassionate until we know how pain feels. *Sympathy* means literally to "feel with" someone.

"You don't know what I'm going through," sufferers sometimes tell us. Their words fly in the face of cheap, superficial attempts at consolation. But if such talk were completely true, human existence would be but sad isolation. No one could relate to anyone else unless he or she had exactly the same firsthand experiences as the other.

"You couldn't understand" may be a sign of pride and self-pity that lead us to believe, because we see only ourselves, that no one could have suffered as much as we suffer.

Others may not have suffered the same evil, but we all have experienced evil, different in kind or degree perhaps, but still evil. We also experience pain second-hand through art, movies, documentaries, and by simply being with and listening to the testimony of a sufferer. In our times of pain, we must beware of the arrogance and resentment that lead us to say, "Stay away from my pain; you couldn't know what I'm going through."

Something in me would like to believe that I have been singled out for suffering, that I am the only person to have pain like this. Suffering makes me vulnerable, weak, dependent, yet I do not want to be dependent upon others; I do not want to "turn and become like children" (Matthew 18:3). And yet, does not the Gospel claim that acknowledgment of such vulnerability, dependence, and weakness is the beginning of our salvation?

We hang on lonely crosses of pain, feeling aloof, heroic, or self-pitying, only to be surprised by the One who climbs up, fits his nail-pierced hands into ours, and takes his place beside us.

We must also guard against avoidance of the sufferer. A tragic dimension of modern life is the detachment of sufferers from their families, friends, and faith communities into isolated enclaves of pain—hospitals, nursing homes, treatment centers. We must fight this tendency by remembering Jesus' words, "I was sick and you visited me" (Matthew 25:36).

How many times do we avoid the sufferer by saying, "I didn't know what to say. I didn't want to make her feel worse"? Let us honestly admit whom we are really protecting. Our own sense of vulnerability, our fear of our mortality, and the maintenance of our delusions are the main blocks to true compassion. We avoid contact with the sufferer lest we "catch" what afflicts him or her—namely, awareness of finitude, vulnerability, and dependency.

We "love as he loved us," by *being there*.

Being there, sharing in the grief, facing the pain and anguish are consoling. But we should remember that Christ not only offered himself, he also offered the truth, words of consolation and hope. Our hope is based not simply upon the feelings of God but upon the Word of God.

Unmerited, deep suffering calls forth our compassion and empathy. It also calls us to testify to "the hope that is in you" (I Peter 3:15). The great, hopeless situations of life call our attention to the aspect of the human condition that poses the questions to which the Gospel is the answer.

It is bracing to say that present suffering is a mystery, but the world is graudally pressing toward betterment. We should therefore not speculate on some other world but nobly accept the world we have. This is the thought of the smug, complacent, well-fed, well-housed, Western mind. It is easy enough for me to be content with things as they are. But what of the child who perishes of hunger in the Ethiopian desert, the millions who starve or die of disease, in constant misery? Is God's good will for their lives finally defeated by human evil?

"Dr. Marney, tell us what you believe about eternal life," we asked Carlyle Marney when he visited our college for Religious Emphasis Week.

"I won't talk with you about that," was Marney's curt reply.

"Why?" we asked.

"Because," he said, "there you are at nineteen or twenty, never having known indigestion, heartburn, impotence, defeat. So what can you know of death? Come back at forty-five and we'll talk about eternal life with integrity."

When we put ourselves in the right place in regard to suffering, that is, where Jesus placed himself—beside those who suffer—we are compelled to ask eternal, fundamental, cosmic questions for which the Resurrection was God's answer.

Christ not only bore suffering on the cross, he triumphed over it. He not only descended to hell; he ascended into heaven. He was raised. Christian hope is not merely hope for gradual betterment, nor is it hope that exists because of the kindhearted but essentially impotent empathy of God. It is hope for a changed world. Not hope for an improved world, but for "a new heaven and a new earth" (Revelation 21:1), where God "will wipe away every tear . . . and death shall be no more, neither

174

shall there be mourning nor crying nor pain any more" (Revelation 21:4).

We cannot specify the exact contours of this hope of a new heaven and earth, but we can say that whatever good is wrestled from suffering is an earthly foreshadowing of the divine bringing of good out of evil. Suffering is to be not passively endured but actively rebuked in the name of Jesus. Every triumph of good over evil is a foretaste of the eagerly awaited "new heaven and new earth," a present experience of the future hope that "neither death, nor life, nor angels, nor principalities, nor things present, nor things to come . . . will be able to separate us from the love of God in Christ Jesus our Lord" (Romans 8:38-39). If God was willing even to suffer crucifixion, we know that human wickedness cannot stump divine resourcefulness.

Every time we pray "thy kingdom come, thy will be done," we do so out of our knowledge that God cares and acts. Each Sunday, as we intercede for sufferers, in this holy act of offering names to God, we name them not to tell God what to do but to open ourselves to what God has done and is doing, to name before God those whom Jesus names as his beloved sisters and brothers in pain. The church that intercedes for the cancer victim is also the church that supplies the hot meals and changes the bandages.

Whoever asks why God permits suffering, such as the suffering of Willie Earle, must also ask why God has allowed our suffering to afflict himself. If we pity ourselves in our contact with suffering and the sufferer, how much more should we pity the God who embraces far more suffering than we can comprehend? If we are looking for this God, so the story goes, we must seek God in suffering—our own and others'—as the One who dwells not in heaven above, but in anyplace of appalling pain. Out by the slaughter pen on Highway 63 on a cold February night, there is God.

One of the great contributions of Judaism is the belief

175

that God not only speaks, but that God also listens. Yahweh is in conversation with creation. Yahweh answers our cries of pain. Jesus is the supreme communicative event of this dialogue. In his story is our hope, a confidence that, in spite of our suffering, "in everything God works for the good, with those who love him" (Romans 8:28) and that even on our lonely crosses of pain, "we are more than conquerors through him who loved us" (Romans 8:37).

TWELVE
IMPLICATIONS FOR THE CONTEMPORARY CHURCH

I hope it is evident that these thoughts on evil have arisen not only out of my story as a person growing up in Greenville but also out of my story as a pastor. Pastors are placed in an either/or position in regard to evil. One doesn't visit the hospital every day or listen to the stories of broken marriages, unfulfilled hopes, loneliness, and anguish without either denying or confronting evil.

"People are basically good. The church exists to help their goodness flower," said a pastor the other day. I do not understand how anyone in the pastoral ministry could believe that—except that pastors, no less than their parishioners, are fearful to face facts.

André Malraux once asked an old priest, "What have you learned in forty years of hearing confession?"

"That people are more miserable and less good than they first appear to be."

Some time ago, I spoke to a group of seminary professors of pastoral counseling on "Theological Aspects of Divorce." In my talk, I suggested that divorce was an occasion for the church to offer forgiveness since divorce, the breaking of a promise, was a sin.

There was a great outcry. "I've known wonderful people who have divorced," said one counselor.

177

"Are you going to tell a woman who divorced her abusive husband that she is a sinner?" another asked.

The group rejected the idea that divorce was sinful. Divorce was a form of bereavement, they said, grief because of "the death of a relationship" rather than anxiety caused by sin.

What troubled me in our conversation was not their views on divorce (in spite of the teaching of Jesus and the church), but their inability to admit to the possibility of sin. I agree to the error of a church making divorce unforgivable, but divorced people sin, married people sin, single people sin. A broken promise is wrong. It is a moral matter. A sin.

The attractiveness of the counselors' notion that divorce is a psychological problem of unresolved grief (rather than a moral matter) is that it rationalizes our behavior. Your therapist tells you that you feel grief rather than guilt.

"I get the impression that you could not admit to the presence of sin in any human activity," I said. At first, I thought they had simply explained sin and evil away because it didn't fit into their psychotherapeutic theology— God the affirming Rogerian therapist.

Later I concluded that the problem was not an inability to admit to sin, but a loss of belief in God's grace. When a church loses confidence in the absolute, transcendent grace of God, what can it do for us suffering souls other than rationalize our sin, moralize about our behavior, and keep assuring us that we are basically nice people who are doing the best we can? Without a story of redemption, if we are not doing our best, we are damned.

My parishioners, in their sin in divorce, marriage, or whatever state they find themselves, tell me that they feel guilty. Despite all the good reasons for their behavior, they feel guilt. It is as if they have violated someone or something, have broken a relationship. The good that they would do they have not done. In short, they sin.

As Celia asks her therapist in T. S. Eliot's *The Cocktail Party*,

> It's not the feeling of anything I've ever *done*,
> Which I might get away from, or of anything in me
> I could get rid of—but of emptiness, of failure.
> Towards someone, or something, outside of myself;
> And I feel I must . . . *atone*—is that the word?
> Can you treat a patient for such a state of mind?

We are, in Scott Peck's phrase, "people of the lie," building layer upon layer of self-deception, fearful to be honest, fleeing the light of self-exposure, the voice of conscience. No one need send us to hell; we are there, trapped in a web of self-delusion and dishonesty, victims of evil rather than victors.

The paradoxical affirmation of Christianity is that our admission of the presence of evil keeps evil from getting out of hand. Unable to confront our evil, we project, scapegoat, deny, rationalize, and destroy, sacrificing others—the Willie Earles of our lives—rather than our delusions. The taxi drivers killed Willie Earle in an attempt to destroy what they hated in themselves. We commit evil in order to be good. That's why some of the most evil people are likely to be found in church—what better way to escape evil than to hide among the good? Can this be why some church people seem so hostile when confronted with the possibility of their own evil? They are here to avoid rather than to encounter.

Yet it is my observation that the church is a dangerous place for those who deny evil. The church is a community of myth, story, tradition, morality. In its own bumbling way, the church stumbles across the truth in spite of itself. People who devote their lives to denying their own imperfection, people who flee those situations where they will be either encouraged to self-examination or subjected to the moral scrutiny of others, will eventually be unhappy in church. Sloth is one of the seven deadly sins which the church battles.

179

Indeed the church could be characterized as that body of people who, in the name of Christ, continually battle evil, fighting it first within themselves, then tackling it in the world. If Scott Peck is right (and I think he is) that "evil arises in the refusal to acknowledge our own sins," then the church is that truthful community which fights lies.

Every time a pastor visits a hospital, he or she should be prepared to meet the enemy. Every time the church is at prayer, it is our acknowledgment that evil is cosmic, persistent, mysterious, and awful. Every time a preacher stands in a pulpit and attempts to be truthful, or a writer puts pen to paper and tries to be honest, or a congregation rises to its feet and sings a doxology, there is our struggle against sin.

Sin is always narcissistic, the result of the "heart curved in upon itself" (Luther), the tragic end of our fatal attempt to be God. So the church—when Scripture is read, when an honest story is told, when a person is baptized—is placing itself at enmity with sin, desperately trying to wrench our gaze off ourselves in order to point us toward God. In so many ways, the church engages its people with the "over-againstness" of God, the otherness of reality. God has made us free to look at the facts or to turn away, so the success of the church is never assured. But whenever someone is converted, "born again" to the blessed and painful realization that we are "dust and to dust you shall return" as well as forgiven, reconciled children of God, the church is about its proper business.

To be a community of truth, the church must be a community of forgiveness. Since we live in an imperfect world, still in the grip of sin, we must cope with our lapses. The kingdom isn't here yet. So we are ensnared in structures of sin over which we have no control. We pay taxes for unjust wars; we work for a political party whose stand on some issues we regard as racist; we accept the money of businesses that exploit the poor. We live under the dominion of sin and evil in the social order as well as in our private lives. No matter how hard we try, we can't avoid a sense of guilt. In fact, those among us who are most opposed to injustice will be those most convinced of our unavoidable entanglement in injustice.

God acts not to condemn us but to forgive, to unclasp the iron bands that enslave the doer to the deed, to unlock the future. Through our confession—in the corporate prayer of confession, through the rites of reconciliation, in our renunciation of sin in baptism and baptism renewal—we articulate our guilt as well as our incapacity to overcome evil on our own. By God's word of pardon, we are freed from the burden of our guilt so that we may return to the front lines.

No one is much good in God's work who is there only to expiate guilt. The burden of guilt renders us weak, defensive, timid, and distracted. So the church offers us the blessedness of another human voice speaking, "Arise, and go in peace, your sins are forgiven."

Without such relief—without this Sunday-to-Sunday reassurance that ultimately it is not all left up to us, that ultimately God is busy in us and in the world—we would despair. Reconciliation is essential to Christian persistence. As Jim White says in *Sacraments as God's Self-Giving*, "Without it, we are only a short-term militia, doomed to slink away in discouragement. But, because of reconciliation, we can enlist for a duration that lasts out our lifetime."

Now do we understand why the church's worship is a movement in the church's campaign against evil? There we receive what we need in order to give what it takes to be in this battle-weary army.

Jesus sent his first disciples to heal and cast out devils (Matthew 10:5-16). He still sends us, giving the church authority to do what he did throughout his ministry. After his Resurrection, he breathed upon his disciples

[margin note: Church that offers (7) – need for reassurance]

181

with the words, "Receive the Holy Spirit! If you forgive the sins of any, they are forgiven; if you retain the sins of any, they are retained" (John 20:23).

One reason that the lawyers hated Jesus was his readiness to pronounce forgiveness of sins, an act that seemed to them a blasphemous usurpation of God's power to forgive (Matthew 9:2-8). The scandal is that the church, that both sinful and saved body, is given this power.

The church is able to be a community of forgiveness because we forgive no sin in others that we have not asked God to forgive in us.

I always tell couples before their marriage, "One good thing about marriage is that it gives you lots of practice in forgiving and being forgiven." Marriage requires forgiveness because any intimate human relationship, any intimate divine-human relationship, can't endure long without forgiveness. So much of our sin is corporate and social.

Our redemption is also corporate and social. On our own, most of us cannot withstand the assault of evil. We get by with help from friends who support us in temptation, underscore our values, call us back to what is true, tell us the Story. The church is also a foretaste of the kingdom, a new human society where suffering, weakness, tragedy, and injustice are viewed differently from the way the world views them. Here is a place to witness "a new heaven and a new earth," not as an isolated club of the elect, but as salt, light, and leaven to a dark world (Matthew 5:13-16; 13:33). Here is a colony, a bridgehead, where, at least in a preliminary way, "every rule and every authority and power" will be destroyed and Christ is putting "all his enemies under his feet," including that dreaded "last enemy" we have spent so much of our lives in bondage to—death (I Corinthians 15:24 ff).

Alcoholics Anonymous is a good illustration of the necessity of community in our struggles with evil. The

182

worse the sickness, the more severe the depth of the evil, the more radical the cure. The A.A. group, in what can only be described as "tough love," leads the individuals to admit that "we were powerless over alcohol," that "our lives had become unmanageable." Then came infamous "Step Four"—"We made a searching and fearless moral inventory of ourselves."

No such inventory could be attempted without the group. A church which is little more than a loose conglomeration of essentially self-interested individuals, half-heartedly committed to discovery of the truth either of Jesus or of themselves, is unlikely to be helpful in making moral inventories of self or society, much less in finding a cure. Too many contemporary pastoral prophets envision themselves as moral Lone Rangers—riding into town, shooting things up with their diatribes, firing at this or that evil, and then disappearing into the sunset, leaving the people on their own. This pastoral style elicits little more than defensiveness. A better way might be to do the tough pastoral work of building a community strong enough to face the truth.

The Practice of Ministry

The pastor who serves this community of forgiveness and truth need not be surprised by the loneliness of the ministry. As we have noted, there are deep, understandable reasons why people, even "religious" people (especially religious people) flee the truth and speakers of the truth.

Preaching is the pastoral task in which we try to be honest about the human situation from the perspective of the Christian story. Either we need a God who saves, or we do not. So preaching speaks of why we need to be saved and how we are saved.

Our proclamation need not dwell on evil alone. Indeed, Christian proclamation must begin and end with the

183

grace of God in Christ rather than with human evil. We simply portray evil as a real part of the human condition. Homiletical honesty begins with the preacher. Are our sermons truthful, or are they only reflections of the preacher's personal alienation from the culture and hostility toward others? We preachers sometimes attempt to justify ourselves by pointing to the attempts of others to sinfully justify themselves.

Sermons on the evil of wealth are particularly dangerous. We preachers generally earn less than our parishioners. Often, our salaries protect us from active participation in our society's acquisitiveness. This frees us for sermons on the sin of greed, subconsciously covering our own greed for power over others through homiletical moralizing.

Any prophetic sermon on sin must be an act of witness to the forgiveness of God which the preacher has experienced in his or her sin. The preacher stands in the pulpit as evidence that liberation from our illusions is pure grace, an act of God to make all things right—even preachers. We preach to submit our images and ideas to the searching critique of the cross.

The preacher speaks to the church because of the church's belief that it needs interpretation more than exhortation from its seers and shamans. Lately, liberation theologies urge the church to make *praxis*—action in behalf of the oppressed—the source of our theology. Preachers must not believe this. Their vocation is to offer theory as their *praxis*. The only honest work for the preacher is to elaborate, Sunday after Sunday, what it means to be confronted by the cross, to keep holding up a mirror to himself or herself and to the congregation. This theoretical, theological task is ethical activity of the highest order. To simply be doing, helping, serving, acting is a historic form of escape from the facts. Rather than to be blindly driven, the preacher is to hold up the mirror of truth, the vision of God, to battle with all

184

false consolations, immortality ideologies, and social deceptions.

Christian education is ultimately the knowledge of good and evil. This is not a matter of insufficient information; therefore, most schooling models are of little help to schooling in Christianity. Nor is it a matter of bringing out the basic goodness in us, but rather a matter of learning our utter powerlessness to defeat, on our own, the powers of sin and death that control us.

But most contemporary Christian educators work out of a developmental rather than a conversionist model of salvation. Cognitive structuralists, such as Piaget and Kohlberg, see human beings as having enormous possibilities for good. "Moral development" is emphasized with little awareness for possibilities of "immoral development." The person is seen as an essentially cognitive being who advances, stage by stage, up the moral ladder toward greater moral capacities. Insufficient attention is given to our freedom to make negative moral choices and to have those wrong choices form us in subtle and powerful ways. We are depicted as advancing up a ladder of increasing moral development in which the person becomes more autonomous and individualized. This view is at odds with the biblical notion that it is our lust for autonomy which leads us into immorality.

When we adopt a developmentalist view of morality, moral failure tends to be viewed as underdevelopment of some sort. Immorality is ignorance. If we knew better, we would do better. We don't need conversion, so the reasoning goes. We need education. But if, as we have argued in this book, evil originates within our personalities, within the way we are as human beings—and not solely as a result of social influences or ignorance—then we are dealing with a phenomenon a good deal more complex than mere lack of knowledge and experience.

Not long ago, I gave a lecture at a college. After my lecture, one student expressed bafflement at why I had chosen this setting to talk about the subject of evil.

"I can understand," he said, "speaking to a group of factory workers or deprived people about sin. But folks here are better than that. Everyone here is fairly intelligent. We have refined our reasoning capacities, our ability to distinguish right from wrong; therefore, I don't believe that you could call us 'evil.' "

Most of the atrocities of history were committed by people who were "fairly intelligent" and had "refined reasoning capacities."

We have no evidence that we can think our way into goodness. Power to reason does not lead to the power to be moral; in fact, more often than not, reason is our greatest ally against morality as we rationalize our immorality. While developmentalists attempt to protect themselves from these charges, they come perilously close to identifying goodness with reasonableness.

The Christian story suggests that human sinfulness distorts our reason. Our development does not free us from sin; it only complicates its workings within us. The way to be free from such distortion is through the biblical notion of repentance. Repentance is a reorientation of the self which leaves nothing—reason, emotion, fears, desires—unaffected.

And so Paul speaks of repentance as a kind of death, a sacrifice of the self, a letting-go whereby we submit to the truth we have spent our lives avoiding (Romans 6:1-14). Our sin—our bondage to death—lies in our attempt to avoid death, our anxious attempt to hold on to our lives and to center all value upon ourselves. True moral development involves the breaking of this bondage.

True Christian education provides us with images that point us beyond ourselves and our anxious self-preoccupation to what is real. It involves submision to the truth. It involves the promise that God's love is stronger than our fear of the facts, that God's grace is eternal and persistent. True Christian education also involves treating one another in a moral manner—being respected as persons who are loved and valued by God and who therefore deserve to be loved and valued by the people of God.

If our Christian education is to be more than simply one more means of avoiding truth, then we must search for ways to be a more graceful community where people are encouraged—through sermons, classes, the liturgy, sharing groups—to face the truth that saves.

I suppose few areas of pastoral work bring someone into more intimate contact with the darker side of human mystery than *counseling*. Exposure to the raw edges of misery and the victims of evil is one of the greater pastoral burdens. I used to tell seminarians, "When you get out of here, in your first parish, get close to an alcoholic. Counsel that person; work with him; stay up one night with him; scold, plead, bargain with him; above all try to help him. That experience will do more to chasten your liberal, naive theology than anything I know."

The complexity of human perversity is nowhere more evident than when we really enter into someone else's life and attempt to help. At the same time, the depth of divine grace is nowhere more dramatic than when we see healing take place in spite of great odds against it.

I agree with Scott Peck's assertion in *The Road Less Traveled* that "mental health is an ongoing process of dedication to reality at all costs." But most of us will not take the perilous road toward wholeness because it requires too much effort and courage. So we remain entangled in our web of self-deceit, dangerous to the health and welfare of others, dangerous to ourselves.

Unfortunately, our counseling often is an ally in the self-deceit rather than an enemy. Rogerian humanistic psychology said that low self-image rather than sin is our problem. I'm OK and you're OK. Self-affirmation is our salvation. The goal of counseling is to build "ego

Counseling

strength" in order to enable someone to affirm himself or herself: the little-engine-that-could psychology.

Curiously, Rogerian views of the self persist, despite a mass of scientific evidence that confirms the biblical view that our problem is exactly the reverse—we are victims of what has been called a "self-serving bias." We invariably take a more optimistic view of ourselves and our behavior than is justified by the facts. We are more often victims of a superiority complex than an inferiority complex. The atrocities of Nazism were not rooted in German feelings of inferiority and defeat, but in Aryan pride and arrogance. Genuine feelings of inferiority are rare in the human being. Pride continues to be the root of the seven deadly sins.

The church may be the one place where people learn from their wounds, claim their weaknesses as their strength. Strong people are not those who must appear to be self-sufficient and righteous, but those who are strong enough to admit that they are neither self-sufficient nor righteous. Here we gain our lives by losing them. True self-esteem is the gift of being valued by God.

True humility is not self-contempt. It is more like self-forgetfulness, freedom from self-obsession, the result of turning away from ourselves to look at something, someone greater than ourselves. So pastoral counseling is a personal, intimate way we attempt to look at ourselves and our problems accurately, a way which would be impossible were it not for the confidence that we do so under the promise of divine grace.

Finally, an awareness of our sin and evil has implications for the *social action* of the church. The same tendencies which we see in individuals are writ large on society as a whole. We are both individuals of the lie and societies of the lie. Christian social ethics has traditionally been described as "the restraint and remedy of sin." This formula describes how Christians view all social arrangements, governments, and economic structures.

Presumably, if the Christian notion of original sin were not true, we wouldn't need laws, traffic lights, and courts; nor would we need to change our laws, economies, and social arrangements. Some social institutions are sinful and need to be changed, but only the incurable romantic feels that restraint is unnecessary.

Yet because we believe in the pervasiveness of sin in all human activity, including law making, statecraft, and economics, Christians are compelled to take a critical view of existing institutions as well as plans for their overthrow or modification. We should be more interested in social visions which promote just arrangements within this world than in utopias, remembering the murderous propensity of all forms of this-worldly messianism. If we compute the minimal estimates of murders committed by Stalinist and Maoist regimes, we conclude that this particular form of political messianism has killed the largest number of human beings in this century, possibly in all history. Few activities are as inimicable to human life as political programs (of the Right or the Left) parading as religious ideals. Absolute power, whether given to government or to the people, corrupts. Righteous indignation, particularly among governments and revolutionaries, seems to be especially demonic, so the church will find itself standing apart from the defenders of either the status quo or the revolution. The church has the rather unpleasant vocation of being the prophetic minority that sees truth and falsehood in both liberators and tyrants. Knowing both conservatives and liberals are equally intolerant of criticism, the church can expect to be condemned by both.

The kingdom of God is not of this world. The Christian is called to alleviate human misery and to resist oppression as a moral imperative, not as acts that bring closer the eschaton. We feed the hungry, clothe the poor, lift up the downtrodden, not as a social strategy but in

189

obedience and thanksgiving to our Lord, knowing that these "little ones" are at the heart of God's kingdom in the future and in our glimpses of it today.

We Christians cannot be passive in the face of evil. Wherever children of God starve, or are naked, ill-housed, persecuted, there is our Lord. Will we be there with him or will we dispassionately sit on the sidelines, calmly note the evil, and enjoy the material benefits that come to the oppressor without actively resisting oppression? Nonviolent resistance is truth telling at its best, pastoral care to both friend and foe, education for the oppressor and the oppressed. It is worship in spirit and truth.

Neither pure "free enterprise" nor pure socialism takes adequate account of our sin. Because people are capable of occasional acts of true goodness, justice does occur in society. But because we sin, societies must be organized to take account of our evil.

THIRTEEN

THE END OF THE STORY

It is important for me to tell my story as one who has grown up in Greenville, to tell the whole story honestly—including the part about the lynching of Willie Earle— because here is the necessary way station on my journey toward wholeness and holiness.

Sometimes we lie about our stories, tell only the parts that make sense or fit neatly into the picture or philosophical scheme of who we wish to God we were. I say, "I am an American," and think of Pilgrims at Plymouth, Jefferson's Declaration of Independence, Bunker Hill, the Gettysburg Address, the Marshall Plan. I forget the Salem witch trials, the genocidal campaigns against native Americans, the carnage of the Civil War, Hiroshima, and, of course, slavery and continuing racism. A test of my wholeness will be how honestly and fully I am able to tell my stories.

But what Herculean act of candor enables us to tell our stories with their complex subplots, confusing villains, ambiguous heroes, and unsatisfactory conclusions? As we have said, we usually face the darker side of ourselves and our world with denial, fantasy, and escape, unable or unwilling to admit that we or the world could be in such a fix.

I would like to picture Greenville in the month of May, flowers in bloom, a southern Eden. But was it then or is it now? My alleged childhood innocence was simple ignorance. The same forces that cause me to fear, to lash out in anger, to crouch in my corner in terror, were with me from the first. There was no Eden; it was corrupted before I arrived. The very traits which are so natural in a toddler are the human characteristics we call evil—self-centeredness, fear of the world and other people, lust to be Number One.

I was born mortal. Each day of my life was but a step closer to the end, whether I knew it or not. As Augustine said, even as a doctor looks at a sick patient and declares, "He will die, he will not get over this," so one could look over my crib and say, "He will die, he will not get over this."

So there was no "fall" in the sense of some innate human moral imperfection of my ancestors which taints me. My fall was simply my awareness of who I was all along. That shocking discovery in the Greenville Public Library, though it felt like a "fall," was simply the discovery of what it means to be human, a discovery I make nearly every day of my life.

Greenville is no Eden, no paradise when you get to know it; nor is anywhere else. I must not deny the evil of my forebears. Nor must I attribute to them especially evil intentions that led to such wrongs, though some may deserve such judgment. Rather, I must come to the saving knowledge that some of the very worst crimes were committed by people who are very much like me—mortal, ignorant, frightened.

Illusions are all we have to fear. We must do our best to take a full, sober look at the worst. We shall have no humaneness until we understand why we rely upon violence, why we lie, accumulate things, and bow to false gods. It's what Nietzsche meant when he spoke of "the disease called man."

Human self-examination at its best, whether it be conducted through the tools of theology, sociology, psychology, or literature, is an investigation of a lie—the lie which is culture itself, the lie which promises immortality but always, in the end, fails to deliver. What is the lie we are living? How high are the costs of living this lie? Is there any way to be honest and still live?

Though the story I have told in these pages is pathetic, if we have really looked at ourselves at our worst, we are prepared to deal with the question in the back of our minds—wherein is our hope? Are there possibilities for humanity, or not?

Marx was right: It is only through careful analysis of our situation that we can overcome our situation. Unfortunately, Marxist analysis became entrenched in its own ideological framework. It failed to be truly objective, scientific, or analytical, neglecting the psychology of human nature. The tyranny of Soviet Russia and other Marxist failures stand as an empirical reminder of the cost of ignoring the facts.

We have, in this book, granted the truth of what modern psychology and psychoanalysis have discovered —people cause evil out of good intentions, not out of innate wickedness. Mortality is our ultimate problem; all other manifestations which we call sin or evil are simply our heroic but vain attempts to overcome our fear of death. We are frightened animals who attempt to overcome our insignificance in ways that can only bring us to grief.

Freud saw evil as the inevitable consequence of human urges and appetites, the dark result of dark, inner longings. But I believe that our evil arises because we are more than an animal with instinctual appetites and drives; we are humans who build and kill and worship and lie because we are limited creatures with unlimited horizons. Conscious of our limits, we spend our whole lives tugging futilely at the chains that bind us. Our nobility is our undoing. So Ernest Becker could say that human history and its tragedies are the record of "a frightened animal who must lie in order to live. . . . Societies are standardized systems of death denial . . . a succession of immortality ideologies." Can we begin to see human history as one long procession of death-denying mythologies? Adam wants to know and be more than he is. Cain kills Abel because his brother seems greater than he. "Let us make a name for ourselves," humanity shouts at Babel (Genesis 11:4). King David thinks that he is above the moral standards which bind mere mortals. And on the story goes.

The anthropologist might tell a different tale with the same moral. So-called primitive people practiced the ritual renewal of nature. By these magic rites, they tried to blend with the ceaseless risings and fallings of the seasons and be as eternal as the cycles of nature. Gradually, as societies became more complex, kings and the military were charged with cosmic powers. The people identified with them, crying "Long live the king!" and merging their claim to immortality in this larger-than-life hero. Now our identities are absorbed into the state which will endure after we are gone. Though we lose our freedom and our individuality, we gain eternity. With coinage and more complex economic systems, money becomes a power fetish, a way to protect our immortality by passing it on to our offspring. Then Marxism promises another revolution in which a heroic state will end injustice and evil by instituting a utopia where class and economic strife shall end and all shall be merged into the will of the group.

A mob of taxi drivers stand on the outskirts of a southern town and blow the brains out of an epileptic black man in order to put him in his place so that they might be in their place—so that they might have enough power over the elemental forces to live forever.

All these attempts to transcend the human condition

are expressions of natural human expansiveness and the will to transcend our animal limitations. We were created as animals but as animals with eyes set upon places we are not able to go. We sigh for Eden, for that place of eternal blessedness and peace where we are able to be all that we dream of being. The evil we think and do is the result of a misguided exercise of the best that is in us. Our greatest evils are committed as we strain toward our grandest illusions. We sigh for Eden. With feet planted firmly in the mud, we look up and long to fly. The myths of military power, nationalistic prestige, capitalism, and Marxism are inadequate stories on which to base our lives because none is true. All sidestep the truly tragic picture of humanity which is thoroughly animal, utterly finite, and yet created in the image of God.

As a true story, the Christian faith is a critique of all false stories. It holds up the harsh mirror of truth and demands that we look at human nature for what it is. Old Testament and New, the biblical story is one long, prophetic judgment upon idolatry. In place of all fanciful perceptions of reality, the Bible bids us attend to the empirical facts. Beneath the surface of all our fears lies the basic fear that we are not God, that we shall die, that from dust we have come and to dust we shall return.

With skillful artistry, the Bible tells the tragic tale of the first brothers, which is also the story of the first murder. With subtle comedy, it describes the first utopia as a Tower of Babel. We hear of Moses rebuking an arrogant dictator named Pharaoh; of a liberated people who, no sooner than they are liberated, enslave themselves to a golden calf. There is Nathan standing before mighty King David and, with a little story, exposing the king's impotence. The Prophets rebuke our armaments, our kings, our economies, even our liturgies and solemn assemblies as vain and false idols that cannot save us.

Self-knowledge is so difficult because it involves the revelation of how our self-esteem has been constructed. It

195

strips our false gods naked and makes a spectacle of them. The story of our self-deception, the Bible indicates, is not so much a record of unrelenting human perversity but rather a long tragedy.

How else does one describe the exploits of this creature who is so wormlike, standing out by some slaughter pen on Highway 63 with shotgun in hand; and yet is so godlike, risking self-destruction in behalf of justice and behaving heroically in countless everyday stands against evil—except as tragedy?

The Bible is, first, a story about God. But it is also the story of humanity which is, even in its wormlikeness, the image of God. Humanity is built like God not so that it shall be eternally frustrated by its distance from God but so that it might know, implanted within its animal consciousness, that it has been created for communion. Our hearts are restless until we find rest in the One who is the source of our life. This is our destiny—not oblivion but communion. Through the ages, Christianity says, we have strained forward, constantly reaching out to the eternal yet always finding it beyond our reach. So, to our surprise, on a cold night in Bethlehem, the eternal reached out to us, became one of us so that we might become one with the eternal. Through the ages we built our grand illusions out across the chasm of great, dark, unmentionable death, never succeeding in bridging the gulf to the infinite. So, on a Friday noon, outside Jerusalem, a cross was raised and infinite love climbed up on it, embraced death, triumphed, and showed us the way to freedom.

This is the surprising story that makes honesty possible. If we are dishonest about human evil and wormlikeness, we are equally dishonest about our godlikeness. For we can't bear to be both human and divine. We would rather revert to the brutish existence of the unknowing beast who is born, eats, procreates, and dies, blissfully oblivious to anything beyond the moment.

Our bestiality is our way of denying our godlikeness as surely as we deny our mortality.

What is man that thou art mindful of him,
    and the son of man that thou dost care for him?
Yet thou hast made him little less than God,
    and dost crown him with glory and honor.
Thou hast given him dominion over the works of thy
    hands;
    thou hast put all things under his feet. (Psalm 8)

Christianity challenges us to overcome both denials—our denial of our finitude and our denial of our divinity. It faces our central problem—death—not with pie-in-the-sky-by-and-by platitudes, but by pointing us beyond our fears to the One who is the source of life.

To see God as Father, Mother, Creator, and Friend is to see our Redeemer and thus to live unafraid of death, trusting the Creator and rejoicing in our part in his creation. My main task, as one witness to the Gospel, is to be attentive to this vision in my own life and then bid others to look at the vision with me.

Alas, let us Christians be honest. Rather than attending to our proper vision, we have often succumbed to false visions so that what we see is not much different from what the world sees. We subscribe to "theologies" that substitute Marxist utopianism for orthodox Christianity. We cut the world down to our size and empty it of the holy. Our churches participate in the idolatry of possession, display, and consumption. We build our buildings big enough and impressive enough to compete with the world's images of greatness. The Moral Majority on the Right is one with many Christian social activists on the Left who forsake the Gospel way of love and suffering for the world's way of coercion and violence—military and legislative—substituting worldly wisdom for Gospel foolishness. We are thus entrapped in the same forces that cause evil—impotence, meaninglessness, and fear and denial of death. No wonder the world has difficulty taking us seriously.

Christianity, when it is true to its message, offers a way to overcome our exaggerated fears of life and death, to find meaning which is not solely of our own creation. Life and death are in the hands of a beneficent Creator. Any human claim to immortality is based on an overflowing of the Creator's eternality upon the creature. We need not—nor in the final analysis, can we—create meaning within our human societies, institutions, symbols, and systems. The significance and meaning of our lives come as a gift. It is futile to try to free ourselves from other evils and social injustices while the fear of death remains in the human heart. We cannot stop exploitation or tolerate the equality of others while we are anxious about our own lives. The only salvation worth having is salvation from the fear of death. Only God can free us.

Observing the 1983 March on Washington, I, like Martin Marty, was struck by the contrast between that march and Martin Luther King's of twenty years earlier. In 1983, the concern was how to get one political party out of power and thus bring in the kingdom. In 1963, Martin Luther King's dream was to change the heart of a nation in order to accomplish social change. Politics alone doesn't change hearts.

While criticizing leftist attempts to impose change through various coercive means, the Christian faith gives little comfort to those rightists who teach that human limitation is built into all things and nothing can change. Christianity is a corrective rather than a substitute for social activism. Christianity *is* social activism, a vision that turns the world of the leftists and rightists upside down. While it offers a profound theological and psychological commentary on the tragedies of the human condition, the follies of history, and the limitations of humanity, this resurrection faith declares that Almighty God is on the side of justice, that good shall triumph over evil, and that God is working out his purposes among us—purposes which shall not be defeated by the powers of sin and death.

Contemporary Christian evangelicals often limit their definition of sin to personal, individual sins. Contemporary Christian social activists often accentuate only the systemic, social sins. Christianity exposes both psychological and systemic bondage and then points the way to our true freedom.

This is one reason why Christianity has a stake in keeping a society open with as free a flow of self-criticism as possible. Humanity has nothing to fear from being honest. From our point of view, the test of a society would be the extent to which it admits its own fear of death and questions its own systems of death denial.

In 1983, when the world was shocked by the shooting of an unarmed passenger jet by the Soviets, we noted that Soviet leadership was incapable of admitting mistakes, errors, or wrongdoing. As they see it, to admit to wrong in such a case would mean that their whole system, their whole society was wrong. This may seem like a childish point of view, and it is. But the denial was more significant. It was the result of a society built upon illusion, an illusion propped up by raw military force. Of course, there is no way to prop up illusion other than by violence. So we might add that the test of a society would not only be the extent of its self-criticism but also the extent to which it relies upon police or military coercion to preserve itself.

In a democracy, self-criticism, satire, and debate are means of exposing our immortality ideologies. Authoritarians scoff at the way in which a democracy seems forever intent on discrediting itself. Totalitarian states value secrecy almost as much as they value military power. Therefore, in any totalitarian state religion, criticism, satire, art, science, even humor are carefully controlled lest these means of human self-transcendence show us for who we really are. But let us quickly add, lest social reactionaries take comfort, that the Gospel not only offers a critique of various proposals for human betterment, exposing illusions; it also offers a scathing rebuke of all social systems and structures that victimize people. Honesty is the first step to freedom. But it is only the first step. The Christian faith is not merely a philosophy; it is a way of life. For us, the truth is a person, personal. It is a way of life in relationship to Jesus Christ who did the truth. We don't merely observe the truth or calmly note the falsehoods we see around us; we follow the truth, attempt to embody the truth even as Jesus himself was the embodiment of truth and righteousness.

> Not every one who says to me, "Lord, Lord," shall enter the kingdom of heaven, but he who does the will of my Father who is in heaven. On that day many will say to me, "Lord, Lord, did we not prophesy in your name, and cast out demons in your name, and do many mighty works in your name?" And then will I declare to them, "I never knew you; depart from me, you evildoers." (Matthew 7:21-23)

Christian preaching is prophetic whenever it honestly exposes our sin and delusions and then invites us to participate in the revolutionary work of the Risen Christ who, by his presence in our world, is forever defeating false gods and raising up for himself a people and a kingdom made up of the poor, the powerless, the sick, the victimized, the hungry, and the wretched of the earth.

To be a Christian does not necessarily mean obligation to make the world a better place. But it does mean obligation to point, in word and deed, to the coming reign of God among the nations, the advent of a kingdom which knows no boundaries—a kingdom based upon truth rather than violence, a kingdom which transcends our visions of what ought to be and turns our values upside down. To be a Christian means not only to point to the kingdom but to participate in the first wave of that kingdom, the first faltering assembly which we call the church. The church is called to be a paradigm, an example of a society which the world considers impossible, a witness to the truth that God—not human power—controls the destiny of the world.

In the church we pioneer those social systems which the world considers to be impossible. The church is a sign, a signal to the world of the way things are moving now that God is among us. This puts our questions of church life into a new perspective. Are we merely duplicating evil, death-denying, and illusion-protecting relationships in the church, or are we providing a countercultural alternative, a revolutionary "colony of heaven," a monkey wrench thrown by God into the machinery of the world?

> I do not pray that thou shouldst take them out of the world but that thou shouldst keep them from the evil one. They are not of the world, even as I am not of the world. . . . As thou didst send me into the world, so I have sent them into the world. (John 17:15-16, 18)

Christians are in the world in a way which is similar to our Lord's way—honest about the "principalities and powers" and their grip over human life, equally honest about the greater power of God who is working to bring all things unto himself. To be honest about our limitations as well as our possibilities is a challenge. The Christian faith offers a way for us to be both honest and hopeful because it is a story of a God who doesn't let go, a God who forgives. Its story is a tragedy, a paradox as accurate and complex as life itself, a comedy as disarming and surprising as God.

Christians are those who live this story, seek to embody it in their lives, witness to it, work in the light of it, and institutionalize it as best they can.

Bill Holmes tells the story of a group of people who found themselves trapped in a room with locked doors. They struggled in vain to open the doors. They tried everything, but to no effect. They were trapped.

A young man stood up in their midst and proclaimed, "There is no way out, but we can live right here anyway."

They were enraged. No way out? Impossible. How dare he try to quench our hope? Still, he told them, "There is no way out, but we can live right here."

"Enough!" they shouted. They rose up in anger; they mocked, beat, and killed him.

Years went by. The people eventually fell in love, laughed and cried, married and bore children. They employed someone to teach their young and someone else to tell them stories. They grew up, grew old, propagated themselves, and died through a score of seasons.

Someone remembered the young man and told the story of him and his stark message.

"You know, he was right," they said. "There was no way out. But we were able to live right here anyway."

"Thou turnest man back to the dust," cries the Psalmist. "You are dirt and to dirt you shall return," writes the Yahwist. Who among us can live with such honesty? How is it possible to survive such cold truth?

"And the Word became flesh and dwelt among us, full of grace and truth; we have beheld his glory, glory as of the only Son from the Father. . . . And from his fulness have we received, grace upon grace" (John 1:14, 16). The Word looks down upon us, from every cross we have placed him upon, and says, to our surprise, "Brothers and sisters, I love you still."

The Triumph of Goodness

Driving through Greenville with my young son one hot afternoon, I was suddenly aware that he was singing—singing some simple tune he had learned in school, no doubt. I listened more carefully:

He walked for you and me all over this land,
He walked for you and me all over this land.
Martin Luther King was a great, great man,

He walked for you and me all over this land.
Martin Luther King was a brave, brave man,
He died for freedom's cause to save this land.

Here I am at the end of my story, an old story of
violence, defeat, hate, and death, a story of lost innocence
and the fall from a primal state of purity that never really
was. I have tried honestly to tell this story.

But this is also the story of One who made our fate his
own, the One who died, predictably, but then rose most
surprisingly. We haven't told our story until we tell his
story and the stories of all those martyrs such as Martin
Luther King who have died because of our sin only to rise
in spite of it. They mock our cynicism and despair and
remind us that, where God is at work, all things are
possible, even the salvation of people like us.

Ronald Goetz makes a helpful distinction between the
thought of Martin Luther and his namesake, Martin
Luther King. Like all the Reformers, Luther stressed
perennial human sinfulness. Humanity is deeply corrupt
and fallen; only God can save. Sometimes in our history,
this deep Protestant sense of sin and human dependence
on God has carried with it a deadly potential: A strong
sense of sinfulness can become a self-fulfilling prophecy.
If I treat my neighbor as the sinner I know myself to be,
my neighbor will not disappoint me. Humanity will live
down to the vision we have of it.

Martin Luther King, Goetz says, was probably the
greatest expression of *American* Christianity. While he
stood in the tradition of Martin Luther, taking sin
seriously and prophetically acknowledging the effects of
personal and social evil, he did not share Luther's utter
pessimism. Like many other American Christians, he
believed that God's grace can lead to true justice. When
King battled racism, he always did so with a vision that
racists, from North and South, both liberal and conservative, were better than their actions. Eventually, our
whole nation responded with actions that were better

203

than we were as we tried to live up to King's dream of redeemed human nature.

At the beginning of this book, I said that American Christianity is often naïve in its belief in human progress and goodness. We are sinners. But we are also *redeemed* sinners. If the American church holds to that awareness, it has something to offer the world in the name of Christ.

Here I am and there you are. Trapped, dying, living under the shadow of the mushroom cloud, lives full of vain illusions of goodness and immortality; dying again and again under a hot southern sun in an Eden defiled, with ghosts of Willie Earle and all the others to haunt and accuse us.

Here I am in Greenville, South Carolina, among folk who killed Willie Earle and then went free. And yet, less than four decades later, I am reminded by the song of a seven-year-old that grace abounds even here, that God's good purposes are not stumped by even the worst of human sin.

Finally, when all is said and done, the presence of evil is most notable as a grand occasion to boldly proclaim the reign of God, a God who climbs up on a cross and turns it into a sign of the ultimate triumph of goodness.

INDEX

INDEX